Ready or No.

 EDITION

Inside you'll find:

by
Suzanne Arnold
Ph.D. Florida State
University
Educator and counselor
for the aged

Jeanne Brock
Adult educator and aging
specialist

Lowell Ledford
Florida Department of
Education

Henry Richards
Older workers specialist
Florida State Employment
Service

Shirley Wile
Consultant, Ready or Not
Professor of Educational
Gerontology and
Retirement Planning
University of Wisconsin

This publication is designed to provide accurate and authoritative information in regard to the subject matter covered. It is sold with the understanding that the publisher is not engaged in rendering legal, accounting, or other professional service. If legal advice or other expert assistance is required, the services of a competent person should be sought.—*Declaration of Principles jointly adopted by a Committee of the American Bar Association and a Committee of Publishers.*

Copyright © 1995 by Elizabeth M. McFadden, Twenty-Second Edition
Published by Manpower Education Institute. All rights reserved.
Manufactured in the United States of America

Manpower Education Institute • 715 Ladd Road, Bronx, NY 10471 • (718) 548-4200

HOW DO I STAND?

READY OR NOT

(Yes) (No)

- ☐ ☐ I know approximately what my social security income will be in retirement.
- ☐ ☐ I know my pension benefits in retirement.
- ☐ ☐ I have a financial savings plan for retirement.
- ☐ ☐ I know approximately future income from my investments— IRA and savings.
- ☐ ☐ I have completed a net worth statement.
- ☐ ☐ I have analyzed my cash flow—monthly and yearly.
- ☐ ☐ I have discussed finances with my spouse.
- ☐ ☐ I have an up-to-date will.
- ☐ ☐ I have a power-of-attorney on myself.
- ☐ ☐ I have my important papers—including my will—where my family can find them. I have reviewed the papers with my spouse.
- ☐ ☐ I have a regular exercise program.
- ☐ ☐ I had a physical examination in the past year.
- ☐ ☐ I've checked my health insurance coverage, both now and for retirement.
- ☐ ☐ I've checked my home for safety and maintenance.
- ☐ ☐ I've discussed retirement plans—where to live, what to do with time—with my spouse.
- ☐ ☐ I am involved in at least one social activity—politics, volunteer work, civic and church activities.
- ☐ ☐ I plan to continue learning after retirement.

READY OR NOT

You are one of the lucky ones! You have an excellent chance of reaching that moment in life when your life is not dictated by job or family ... when responsibilities that accompanied earlier roles have lessened ... when you are free to choose what you want to do.

How do you feel about this approaching stage of life? If you are like most people, you probably have mixed feelings ... both hopes and fears about what it may mean to your life.

YOU ARE NOT ALONE

However you feel, it shouldn't be lonely. Did you know that over 300,000 people enter the ranks of the aged every year. Did "aged" bother you in the preceding sentence? It should not, because it is your qualification for the benefits described earlier—the good life of retirement.

People are living longer today than ever before. In 1900 life expectancy was 50 years of age. In 1960 the average 65-year-old American could expect to live another 14.3 years. In 1989, according to the latest data available, average life expectancy for 65-year-olds increased to 17.2 years.

The current average length of retirement beyond 65 for a man is 15 years, while the woman can expect to live an additional 18.2 years.

Better health care, shorter work weeks, a higher standard of living, earlier retirement...these factors have contributed to the growing numbers of older people who are around to enjoy what Browning affirmed to be "the best," for which youth has been a preparation.

ARE YOU READY?

What do you know about this new life?
What can you do to prepare for it?
What do you know about yourself?

This handbook, **Ready or Not**, is devoted to the purpose of helping you answer some of the preceding questions. They are designed to convince you that retirement represents an opportunity for a rich and rewarding life, along with some distinctive challenges. Advance preparation can be made to enable you to COPE with problems which may arise. The book suggests a number of ALTERNATIVES for you to consider as you arrive at your own individual plan of action...action to assure that your mature years are indeed **the best years of your life!!**

STAY ACTIVE

Remember how many years you will have ahead if you retire early. Make sure, by advance planning, that you can make them active and busy years. Do volunteer work. Develop hobbies. Become involved in community affairs. Learn to play.

Retire early if you want to and can enjoy your later years more, free of financial worries and free of boredom. **Stay on the job if you desire. Mandatory retirement has been abolished for most workers.**

- **Keep up to date.** Think about attending classes (many are free) at a college nearby or in continuing education programs. The sharpness of a mind is generally blunted not by age but by disuse. If you have a lively mind and an interest in improving it, whatever your age, you almost certainly can find educational opportunities that will open up a world of vast horizons in later years. You'll make new friends—and you won't feel out of place in classes on today's "graying campuses."

TALK IT OVER...

Aging: Did you know that?

- Senior citizens over 65 constitute 10% of the total U.S. population. More than 25 million persons, age 65 years or older, live in the United States.

- The ability to learn new skills and acquire new information remains relatively unchanged from age 20 through age 60. Intellectual powers do not decline as rapidly as people think. "You can't teach an old dog new tricks" is true only if the "old dog" happens to believe this proverb!

- Physical strength is maintained from biological maturity until age 60. Physical strength may be due to factors more related to health than to the number of years a person has lived.

- Comprehension and vocabulary ability holds strong through age 60. Physical dexterity and reaction to stimuli reach a peak at age 18 with a slow decline after age 40. Ability to learn, though, is relatively unaffected by age.

- Social Security and pension plans together account for 60% of the average senior citizen's income.

- Of all married couples over 65, the percentage living in their own households is 80%. For those individuals not married, 50% live on their own.

- The percentage of all persons over 65, living in an institution, is only 5%. Institutions include nursing homes, retirement homes, and mental hospitals.

- The average couple has 25 years of partial leisure after their children are grown.

- 90% of persons over 65 report relative freedom from chronic health problems that could limit their activities. Two factors that are important to extended health and happiness are: (1) an understanding of one's self (physically, mentally, and socially) and (2) good medical care in early and later life.

- About 75% to 80% of pre-retirement income is necessary to enable the retired person to maintain his previous level of spending and living. Some expenses will decrease: work-related expenses (eating out, clothes, transportation) and taxes will be lower. Housing may be lower, depending where you will live. Bad news: inflation will affect buying power and health expenses will rise.

Chapter One

Did you get the message? Old age may not be so grim an experience as you may have imagined. What you think of yourself will have as much to do with what retirement means to you as the number of years you have lived.

Reaching a particular number of years does not automatically convert you into a less valuable person. Your responsibilities have changed ... your "roles" are not the same. BUT haven't you been through several changes in responsibilities and roles before now?

Many women have "retired" from active motherhood ... that stage when individuals depended directly on them for their care. Mothers may be in a position to share insights on "retirement" with fathers who are just now facing the experience.

You cannot do everything you once did. But isn't it true that your interests and abilities have been changing with the different stages through which you have already passed? Haven't you already discovered some of the compensations which are built into life, as expanded interests and capacities replace the earlier concerns and abilities?

WHAT'S GOOD ABOUT OLD AGE?

Nothing?!! Let's be fair. There are some qualities highly prized by society that are frequently found in older people. In what area does age seem to have the poorest chance of competing successfully? In getting a job, right? Did you know that the following characteristics were given by employers as those they would value above youth, strength, and agility?

1. Adaptability
2. Dependability
3. Experience
4. Knowledge
5. Good work habits
6. Good attitudes
7. Pride in work
8. Consistent performance
9. Stability

Will the worker who matches the description given in the above list please stand up... Can it be? It is ... our friend, the older worker!

Question: "If old age is so good, why is it necessary to have a series of programs getting people ready for it?"

Second question: "Why are you proposing solutions where no problem exists?"

We have attempted to present the positive aspects of aging because the negative aspects have received ample exposure. From our youth-oriented culture on the outside to the erosion of self-esteem on the inside, the maturing adult is besieged by assurances that life has passed him by ... he used to be ... he used to do ... but now he isn't ... and he doesn't...

... BUT creative people from across the years parade before our memories to say that being and doing are very much a part of advanced ages ... if you believe in yourself, you have solved some of the most critical problems that some adults face. For you see, people tend to see you as being what you see yourself to be ...

... After all, who has a better right to know?

WHAT'S THE PROBLEM?

The farsighted adult with a good self-concept can cope with his problems. The problems are real, and no attempt will be made to minimize them. Remember, our purpose is to convince you that it's better to be ready than not!

A realistic assessment of the retirement situation and some practical steps taken at your present stage of life can make your future years far richer than you thought they could be. A word to the careless ... POSTPONEMENT and AVOIDANCE have been found to be 100% ineffective in combating the difficulties of advanced years.

TRANSITION is the word that might sum up many of the tensions experienced by older citizens. Consider the following TRANSITIONS:

FROM	TO
Work	Leisure
Greater Income	Lesser Income
Many Responsibilities	Fewer Responsibilities
Established Routine	Unscheduled Time

With INFORMATION about the aging process and a wholesome PHILOSOPHY about growing old, you can attain a satisfying, rewarding life.

If the need to adjust constitutes part of the problem —

WHAT'S THE ANSWER?

Advance planning and the cultivation of those personal qualities which enable an individual to cope at any age will be ingredients in the personal answers you will be developing.

Introduction

You are the largest component in your answer … and you can predict what your performance will be.

How well have you adjusted to earlier stages of development? We can look at any individual's adjustment to life and problem solving and say whether he'll be socially adjusted in later life. For example, a person must be able to:

- have a real, enduring, and honest affection for others
- be independent
- find satisfying outlets
- enjoy life
- develop a sense of usefulness

Sidney Scott Ross, in his book, *How To Enjoy Your Later Years*, suggests that you can clarify your thinking about retirement by deciding if you agree or disagree with the following statements:

	Agree	Disagree
"I feel I'm too old to start anything new."	_____	_____
"Hobbies are for young folks."	_____	_____
"It's almost impossible to make new friends in later life."	_____	_____
"It's good for an older person to break habits occasionally."	_____	_____
"An older person can grow mentally even after he starts to decline physically."	_____	_____

THE TIME TO BEGIN …

- Begin NOW to make your plans for **financial security**.

  If you invest $100 a month at age 55, you will have invested $12,000 in 10 years (by age 65). But remember this: with 7% interest your total investment will be **greater** than $12,000 by a couple thousand dollars.

  If you wait until age 60 and invest $200 a month for 5 years, you will also have invested $12,000.

  However, the total investment (including 7% interest) for this plan is less than the total for the first one discussed—in fact, what you would save at $200 a month is almost half the interest return possible with a 10-year $100 a month

investment. Obviously, it pays to begin early in planning for financial security.

- Begin NOW to make your plans for **health**.

  The symptoms of many diseases and deteriorating health conditions can be detected and corrected through frequent examinations and early treatment.

- Begin NOW to make your plans for **housing and living arrangements**.

  If you plan to live in your present house, you can take steps today to see that your mortgage is paid off before your income is reduced. You can take steps today to investigate alternative sites before the time of retirement is upon you.

- Begin NOW to make your plans for **leisure**.

  Discover today what your interests really are. Acquire today the materials you need to develop a hobby you expect to cultivate in the days ahead. Discover entertainment opportunities and rehearse some of the activities which you think may interest you tomorrow.

- Begin NOW to make your plans for a **second career**.

  You may want to continue working—but at a different job. Maybe own your own business, making money from your hobby. Prepare now!

IT CAN MAKE A DIFFERENCE

You are one of the lucky ones … *healthy* and *wealthy* enough to face retirement … and *wise* enough to plan ahead.

YOU can make YOUR LIFE better. *Remember*, aging, retirement, maturity … they are just ahead … they are coming … **Ready or Not.**

Believe me, if I'd have known this is what you meant when you said we'd travel, I'd never have let you retire.

PLANNING A SOUND FINANCIAL FUTURE

Where do you stand? Are you a young person just entering the business world? At the midpoint of your career? Or rapidly approaching retirement? Wherever you stand it just makes good sense to stop periodically, review your financial status thoroughly, and do some sound and intensive planning for the future. The purpose of this section is to help you do just that.

WHY IS FINANCIAL PLANNING SO IMPORTANT?

That's pretty obvious, isn't it? All of us are looking for a full, active and rewarding life for ourselves (and for our family, if we have one). To provide this kind of life calls for planning, financial and otherwise.

Without planning it's so easy for family funds to be spent in a thoughtless and wasteful way. There's never much left for savings and investment, and necessary but perhaps careless borrowing saddles us with expensive interest obligations.

Such a careless approach to family finances makes life even more difficult as you go along. There are always major financial needs looming up that may further complicate matters:

The need for a new furnace, a new car or a new house; children and their own special needs, often costly ones; the major expenditure required for college educations; and finally, too soon, retirement—often 15 to 20 years of living without that full monthly paycheck.

INFLATION MAKES PLANNING MORE CRITICAL

Inflation is an insidious thing. We know it is happening, but we don't give sufficient attention to the effect it has on every dollar we earn and save. Between 1968 and 1988 we in the United States had some measure of inflation every year varying

---

Note: At the end of this chapter, you will find worksheets for computing your cash flow and your net worth.

---

from 1.5% to a double-digit figure of 13.5%. The real shocker is that in this 20-year period the Consumer Price Index went from 104 to 347.6—*a total increase of 234%.*

The Consumer Price Index for urban workers in 1993 registered only a 2.6% increase, the second smallest increase since 1975. Good news, but even at this low rate, the purchasing power of a 1993 dollar will decline to 48 cents in twenty years. While financial advisors say it costs less to live in retirement—60-70% of preretirement income—if 1993's low inflation rate holds steady, a family with an income of $40,000 today will need a retirement income of approximately $56,000 in the year 2014 to live comfortably. More if the rate of inflation increases.

FINANCIAL PLANNING COVERS TWO IMPORTANT PHASES

A sound financial plan is very important to insure comfortable living for you and yours in the face of continued inflation. This section outlines how to develop such a plan focusing on two important elements:

- Controlling family expenditures by evaluating current spending practices and developing a practical and effective family budget program.
- Insuring an adequate level of future income by setting up a consistent, diversified and balanced investment plan.

STEP ONE: DETERMINING YOUR CURRENT FINANCIAL STATUS

Certainly the place to start in developing a personal financial plan is to determine your current financial status. This involves, first of all, computing your net worth. Your net worth is simply the difference between your assets and your liabilities.

WHAT YOUR NET WORTH TELLS YOU

This computation tells you first of all whether or not your assets exceed your liabilities—and by how much. It also tells you how much of the total value of your assets is represented by each category shown. It provides you with a similar breakdown of your liabilities.

With this information you can evaluate your current financial condition in a thorough and systematic way. Review the figures shown, asking the questions:

- Do I have a major financial problem in that my Assets barely exceed my liabilities?
- Is my life insurance adequate for my family's needs?
- Do I have sufficient money set aside in liquid funds for our current needs?
- Are my investments properly planned and diversified?
- Can I count on being paid the full value of my loans receivable?
- And so forth!

Similar questions can and should be asked about the composition of the liabilities you have listed. They represent in most instances a heavy load of finance charges that should be minimized as much as possible.

GATHERING YOUR FINANCIAL INFORMATION

To start, you get together all your financial papers and reports providing needed information on the family assets and liabilities. Included among these would be such items as: savings records, your checkbooks, statements for CD's, stocks, bonds, funds, etc. and similar reports on your residence, vehicles, mortgages, loans, etc.

Hopefully you have all these papers put aside in one place and organized for easy reference. If they are not so organized, it is certainly a wise thing to correct the situation even if you don't make the net worth computation.

Also it's not really that hard to locate the market value of some of the listed items. Tax reports and records can be helpful, and a check of the classified section of your local paper can give you a good idea of the value of such assets as your home, your cars, tools and equipment, etc.

THE TREND IN YOUR NET WORTH

It is a good idea to perform a net worth computation yearly. Those who do can see how their net worth is growing. In evaluating this growth look for two things:

- A steady growth from year to year.
- A growth rate that exceeds the inflation rate by a substantial amount.

If the growth rate is low or uneven, you should lay this current year's net worth computation alongside last year's computation and determine any areas of weakness. How are your investments growing in value? Your real estate? Are your liabilities being reduced? Your loan indebtedness? Mortgage obligations?

Yes, effective use of the net worth computation and trend analysis is an important first step in getting a stronger understanding of your family's financial condition.

YOUR CASH FLOW

If a look at your net worth (and the trend in its growth—or decline) suggests something needs to be done to improve your financial picture, then the best way to get a precise understanding of the problem is to compare your expenses versus your income in a specific way. The "worksheet for computing your cash flow" will help you do this.

Determining your cash flow shows you whether or not your expenses exceed your income—or vice versa. If expenses exceed income and you are losing ground financially, obviously you need to take some definite corrective action. If, on the other hand, expenses and income balance out, then the question is whether or not sufficient funds are being set aside for savings and investment."

However, let's assume that the totals as shown clearly indicate you are overspending. You will then want to look at the individual items in your expenses listing to determine areas in which the spending problem is centered. Probably these areas will stand out, as they say, "like a sore thumb."

Also very helpful is comparing the percentage of income you spend on each category with a breakdown such as the following budget for the "average" retired couple (according to the Bureau of Labor Statistics):

Housing	33%
Food	29%
Transportation	10%
Medical Care	10%
Clothing	5%
Personal Care	3%
Entertainment & Education	4%
Other	6%

If your percentages vary widely from the above, this is just another clue to the categories in which you may be overspending.

DETERMINING YOUR CASH FLOW

This takes some doing. There's no question about it. So give yourself adequate time to do the job right.

Use the expenses listing on the form as your initial guide taking one category at a time and searching out the needed information. Much of this information can be obtained from your checkbook, your credit card statements or your tax records.

The most difficult information to get is that related to cash purchases. Either estimate these figures from personal experience, or keep a journal on these items for several weeks to establish a pattern.

The income information should be searched out in a similar way using your income statements for reference purposes.

> *Important: Don't expect to achieve perfect accuracy with this analysis. Even an imperfect job will give you a strong starting point for improving your financial status.*

STEP TWO: BRINGING EXPENSES INTO BALANCE WITH INCOME

If you have just completed the cash flow worksheet, you know whether your expenses exceed your income. If it does, then you'll surely agree you need to take some immediate action to correct this imbalance.

Even if your income exceeds expenses, it's still a good idea to evaluate and control family spending practices. Why not do this conscientiously and use the extra funds to further beef up your savings and investments.

Cutting back on expenses is not as difficult as you might think. Most of us—over the years—have let many old-time luxuries become today's necessities. This becomes apparent if we study the different elements of our expenses listing closely. Also "little things mean a lot!" A $20 savings here—$10 there—an occasional $40-$50 savings, total up to $150 to $250 monthly, a tidy sum to help in the balancing process.

EXAMINE YOUR EXPENSES TO REDUCE OVERSPENDING

Look at your listing of expenses (taxes, house, vehicle, etc.). You will see that the list covers practically all the ways you can spend your hard-earned income. So take each category; study it carefully—one item at a time.

Take plenty of time and do a thorough job of evaluating the expenditures made for these items.

Be sure to ask yourself the right questions— questions like these:

- Is this product or service really essential?
- Could we get by with a less sophisticated, less expensive version of the item?
- Are we using more of the product or service than we really need?
- Are we buying at a good, competitive price?

DEVELOP AN ACTION PLAN

You won't get much help out of your review unless you make some decisions and get them down on paper for follow-up. As you study each category, decide what, if any, reduction plan you want to implement and note it under the appropriate heading in the action plan.

Obviously you can't carry out all the reductions at once and some will take longer than others to implement. So prioritize them, putting the most significant reductions first in line. Add a deadline date for completion of each one. This puts some pressure on you to go to work.

At this point start taking the actions called for— handling one item at a time. Take your time and do each job right. Then, as you complete each action, cross it off your list.

When you have completed this balancing of your expenses and income, you will be ready for the next step—setting up your budget.

LIBRARY:
A SOURCE OF INFORMATION

As you go through your listing of expenses you will frequently say to yourself, "I need more information about that"—or—"What are the alternatives to the way we are handling this matter?" This is the study and research part of the job that helps you get the reduction results you want.

There is a source nearby that greatly simplifies any research job—your public library. Books and periodicals cover every conceivable subject— including the ones in your expenses listing:

> *Ideas on how to save on taxes; tips on reducing house mortgage payments; insurance information; buying guide; economy food tips and menus; etc.*

With the help of the librarian you can quickly become an expert at locating whatever you want to know about the elements in your listing of expenses.

MAKE EXPENSE REDUCTION A COOPERATIVE PROJECT

You will probably find that many of the expense reduction measures you decide to take will not penalize anyone in the family. However, if the out-of-balance financial condition is a serious one, more drastic measures must be taken. The decisions reached on such reductions should be mutual ones agreed to with good humor by both husband and wife—with the rest of the family also having input.

ONE LAST BIT OF ADVICE

We've taken the "housing" account and gone through it for you—just as you might do it yourself. Here it is:

"Okay," you might say to yourself, "These are big budget items. Can I save on them starting with the mortgage payments?

"Well, interest rates have been bouncing all around for the past year or so. It may be possible to refinance—cut 2% or more from the interest rate we're paying. Sure there will be some costs involved in the switch but in the long run we may be able to save thousands of dollars on interest charges.

"Also, haven't people been talking about saving money on their mortgage by just 'paying ahead'? I could ask about that too."

Calculating the Difference

Here is an example of the difference between monthly and biweekly payments on a 30-year $50,000 mortgage at 8 percent interest.

	Monthly	Biweekly
Payment	$368	$184
Annually	$4,416	$4,784
Total interest paid until maturity	$82,480	$47,336
Years to maturity	30 years	20 years, 9 months

The next question you'll ask is, "Am I getting the right coverages and a good price on our homeowner's insurance?

"First, I'm going to take a closer look at my policy and be sure I understand all the provisions—and coverages. Check on whether or not they provide just the protection we want: not too little—but not too much either. That's costly. The I think I'll check with a few friends to see wha their homeowner's costs them. Maybe—after I'v done a little research at the library—I'll get a cou ple of proposals from some different insuranc companies too. Might be able to save some mone on the premiums.

"And I'm going to check out carefully the othe house expenditures we make. The little odd job around—maybe I can learn to do more of them myself. And lawn service—and lawn spraying With the new mowers and new liquid fertilizer now available—Junior can probably take ove those jobs.

"Now let's make some notes on these matters i my expense reduction action plan."

Note: If you take every category in your listin of expenses and go through them in this wa you can be sure of this: unless you were th neighborhood's greatest efficiency expert i the first place, you will find a lot of hidde savings possibilities that will help you do yo "balancing act" without fear or pain.

STEP THREE: SETTING UP YOUR FAMILY BUDGET

If you have been developing a financial plan alon the lines we have been suggesting, you have exam ined your spending habits, planned projecte adjustments in that spending pattern, and set up i effect a yearly spending budget by category.

The next step is to put this planned spendin pattern in a budget form that you can use to contro your spending and achieve your financial goals.

WHY A BUDGET IS WORTHWHILE

Besides the obvious advantages of eliminatin waste and controlling expenditures, there are number of additional advantages to living by budget:

- Having a financial guide or budget makes th task much easier and productive. Like follow ing a road map, you reach your objective wit fewer delays and wrong turns.
- You know where you stand financially from month to month—another factor that brings re peace of mind.
- It provides money for that all-important inves ment program that will enable you to mee major expenses down the line (home, childre college, retirement).

SOME OVERALL TIPS

Many people have given up on budgets because they didn't use good judgment in setting them up in the first place. To avoid this, consider the following suggestions as outlined by many financial planners:

● Continue to approach your working budget as a family project with husband and wife—and the children, too—having input. If decisions are not made on a truly mutual and fair basis, family members just won't work to make the project succeed.

● Keep the budget format—and the necessary administration of the program—as simple as possible. As you go along, you may very well find ways to short cut or eliminate unnecessary details or record-keeping. That's fine. Just don't forget your overall purpose—and the importance of "knowing where you stand."

● Plan on the first few months being a trial-and-error period. Evaluate what you are doing carefully—and make your adjustments in allocations and in the way you keep records.

KEEPING BUDGET RECORDS

"Standard budget books" are available at every office supply store. Many of them are well-designed and instructions for their use are spelled out in some detail. Look through these budget books carefully and select the one that suits your preference. One feature in particular to look for is a thorough breakdown and listing of the various possible types of expenditures. You need such a listing so you will know which accounts to charge for all the wide variety of expenses you pay for.

You can also use the format from the cash flow worksheet in this section and set up your own budget record on a columnar pad. However, it's a good idea to refer to one of the "standard books" in set-ting up the category listings, the method of recording information, and the set-up for summarizing expenditures.

MAINTAINING BUDGET INFORMATION

Whatever budget book you select, the format of the monthly record will be reasonably self-explanatory. Also there will probably be a good set of instructions on how to make the necessary entries and computations. However, here are a few suggestions which may further simplify the process for you.

If you look at the budget accounts, you will see it is very easy to obtain much of the information asked for. It is shown either in your checkbook record or credit card statement. It's just a matter of transferring the appropriate information to your budget record once a month. Recognizing the value of a checkbook record as a source of budget information, some people who budget make a point of paying all expenses over $10 or $15 by check.

What is left are the frequent cash purchases for food, entertainment, personal care, etc. Some plan must be set up to keep track of these expenditures. One way is to keep all receipts for such cash purchases, checking to be sure they show clearly the items purchased and the prices paid. Where no receipt is provided, you keep a listing in a notebook you carry for that purpose. With these notes it is easy to update your budget record.

Another way to keep track of small item purchases is what is called in business "the purchase order approach." You simply take the funds you have set aside for something like "meals out" and you spend up to the level provided for. Then you stop spending for that type of item for the month. Try this, and you'll watch your nickels and dimes.

Financial Planning

Of course, it's easy to record the total of these expenditures in your budget book. It's the budget amount shown—or less.

ADMINISTERING YOUR BUDGET

Keeping your budget program working is the last and most important factor involved in the whole process. This starts with a clear assignment of responsibilities.

Who is going to be responsible for keeping the budget records? This must be specified so the job gets done regularly.

How is the responsibility for controlling the different categories of spending to be divided between husband and wife? The cash purchases for food, entertainment, personal care and miscellaneous items are a particular problem here. The two should look at this matter together using recent experience as their guide—and make a detailed list of the specific items for which each will be responsible.

Then, where do you keep the budget funds so they are safe—yet readily available? Some will choose a joint checking account; others a savings account and a checking account. Separate checking accounts are still a third way. With this system an appropriate allocation of monthly income is made to each account to cover assigned budget expenditures. Then each spouse draws on "his" or "her" account as they see fit during the month for necessary cash or to pay current bills by check. Whatever system you decide on, make the plan definite and carry through on the agreed-upon procedure to guard against any misunderstanding between partners.

Finally, there is the very important monthly budget review. This above all determines whether or not your program works. At this review you and your partner check whether or not you are staying within your budget limits. If you are not, you decide what action to take to correct this overspending—account by account. On the other hand if you are underspending in some categories, you can take advantage of this situation by adjusting upward the budget limits in other account categories as good judgment advises.

If you put in a budget program as outlined here, you can be reasonably sure that you are spending your income wisely and in line with your preferences. Also if you have done your planning well, you will know that allocations are being made regularly to your investment account to insure your continued financial security.

STEP FOUR: DEVELOPING A SOUND SAVINGS AND INVESTMENT PLAN

We now move ahead to another important phase of our financial planning. We have set aside funds for savings and investments of some kind. The amount in our budget for this purpose may be small, but hopefully it will increase as we add a portion of our future cost of living and merit pay increases to the funds designated for savings.

At this point, we need to develop a plan for utilizing these funds effectively. Such a plan should provide for current, day-to-day living expenses and the minimizing of credit card and loan debt—and make a start on setting aside money for such major family requirements as: home, children, advanced education, and, ultimately, retirement.

This section covers the alternatives available for such savings and investment purposes and how to structure such a program. It breaks down into three phases in line with the way such a program realistically is developed:

- First phase: setting aside an adequate "working fund" and essential insurance protection.
- Second phase: starting a savings program to provide added financial protection and coverage of future needs.
- Third phase: developing a full blown savings and investment plan.

THE FIRST PHASE: A "WORKING FUND" AND INSURANCE PROTECTION

As the heading suggests, right at the start of your financial planning, you should aim at taking care of two prime financial needs: a "working fund"—and insurance protection. We'll begin with . . .

THE WORKING FUND

Every family needs such a fund. It provides for your day-to-day expenses and also should be big enough to cover such major expense items as needed car repairs, all but the largest appliance purchases, even such emergencies as a temporary lay-off. These funds should be readily available. Still—even at this first stage—you want them to be earning "something" in the form of interest.

The problem of "credit card" and other debt raises its head at this point. Some people seem to think that having a credit card—or two—or more somehow increases their income. Of course, it doesn't—far from it. Rather than saving your money, it costs you a whopping 18-20% in interest each year. Yet the use of a credit card for borrowing purposes becomes a habit. The required monthly payment seems small, and more and more debt accumulates. Having a number of cards and a total credit card balance of $2,000 or more is quite common.

This is a dangerous financial situation. You know it has become a real problem for you when you start to see tell-tale signs such as these. You never have adequate funds to start paying down the balance on your credit cards. You must use a credit card to borrow money to meet day-to-day "consumption" and expenses. You take out a new credit card to borrow money to make the payments on your current cards.

Here's an example that highlights the folly of using credit cards carelessly:
1. Suppose you save $2,000 and put it in a savings account earning 5% interest. You will earn $100 per year on your savings.
2. Suppose, on the other hand, you put aside $2,000 and paid off the $2,000 balance on your credit card statements. You would save—in effect earn—18% on the transaction or $360. That's $260 more than the $100 you would earn on $2,000 in a 5% savings account.

The rule of thumb is to never—never—use credit to pay for everyday living expenses. Use credit instead to buy assets that have long term value: a home, a car, a major appliance that reduces living expenses.

Back to the "working fund." Obviously such a fund helps you avoid excessive credit card and loan indebtedness. The question is: "How much should you have in such a fund?" Financial planners seem to agree you should keep about two-to-three months income in such a fund. That is:
● With a $2,500 monthly income: a fund of $5,000-$7,500

DO YOU NEED A FINANCIAL PLANNER?

Although financial planners can help you make investment decisions, hiring a planner presumes you have discretionary income to invest. Experts say most investments should not be made until you have financed some very basic living items, such as housing, insurance, and a cash reserve fund for emergencies. If you find you cannot meet these (and other) necessary financial requirements, you may decide you need help not in investment planning, but in basic money management.

Whether or not you use the services of a financial planner you must organize by preparing your own net-worth and cash-flow worksheets.

Be informed on financial matters. Your library is a great source and your local educational institutions offer classes. You should do this whether or not you hire a financial planner.

If you have money to invest and decide you need a financial planner, ask how they get paid. **BE CAREFUL.** Some simply are salespersons for products they recommend. Fee-only planners charge a straight fee for their services. Be sure you get a written statement of their charges.

Ask for a sample of a written financial plan.

● With a $3,500 monthly income: a fund of $7,000-$10,500

As to where you keep these funds, the alternatives are probably not unfamiliar to you and are mostly available from your local bank. These bank savings alternatives offer guaranteed security of your funds, if the bank is insured by the Federal Deposit Insurance Corporation and your account totals less than the stipulated limit for liability.

STRUCTURING YOUR SAVINGS

As suggested earlier, you want adequate liquid funds available as needed, but you want to be earning some interest too. So what you do with your "working fund" is divide it between: your checking account, and either a savings account or a money management account.

You keep just enough in your checking to meet your current monthly needs—and the rest in the money management account earning interest. This balance between the accounts you watch closely to be sure you are earning interest on as much of your funds as possible.

INSURANCE PROTECTION

If you're married and have a family, you must realize the need for insurance protection in the event some premature tragedy should happen to you or your spouse. The need for this protection is greatest when you are younger and the insurance benefit must provide income for your family over a long span of years in case of such an untimely event.

The need for such protection should lessen as you grow older. Over the years you and your spouse should build assets that provide income protection in themselves. The children grow up, become independent, and are able to fend for themselves.

Which all means you need to set up your life insurance program early as part of your financial base—and plan the program to provide adequate financial protection particularly at the start.

STRUCTURING YOUR INSURANCE

The type of people you and your spouse are determines to a great extent the type of insurance plan that is best for you:

● If you have the discipline and control necessary to handle such a plan, many financial planners would say you should select an ample "term" policy, putting any additional money that is available into such an investment as a sound mutual fund.

● If you do not feel you have the discipline for consistent contributions to a separate savings and investment program, then you are better off with a universal life or variable life program. With this approach you are in effect forced to make the regular investments as a means of keeping the policy in force.

HOW MUCH PROTECTION?

Few people can afford to buy sufficient insurance protection to guarantee that their families will not suffer a loss of income at the death or disability of the major wage earner. The point is to do the best you can with the money available for this purpose.

INSURANCE OPTIONS

Term Insurance. Term insurance provides the greatest dollar amount of coverage for the least amount of money—$100,000 of protection for just several hundreds of dollars per year. However, the premiums for a specific amount of insurance become greater as you grow older. Since your needs for such protection grow less too, you can reduce the amount of your coverage as you see fit. Term insurance does not build any cash value.

Whole Life. This insurance provides a stipulated death benefit, but it also includes a savings feature, building cash value as the years go by. You can borrow against this cash value; and if you eventually cancel the policy—cash it in, obtaining the savings that have built up. The chief problem with this type of policy is the low rate of interest usually earned in the savings phase of the plan. (Universal life is similar to whole life but ordinarily provides a better return on the savings portion of the policy because of the way the savings funds are invested.)

Variable Life. This type of insurance combines many of the advantages of whole life policies with those of a mutual fund investment. You have guaranteed minimum death benefit as with whole life. However, the savings portion of the insurance is invested in a mutual fund plan (of varying types) that may provide you with greater growth and appreciation.

The first thing to do in this matter is to consider what income the family would have considering such factors as:

The earning ability of the surviving spouse; the current state of the family finances; the possibility and level of Social Security benefits.

Then you set up your insurance plan to come as close as possible to the monthly income needed for reasonably comfortable living.

DISABILITY INSURANCE A MUST

You're twice as likely to be disabled for 90 days as to die before age 65. Yet fewer than half of all working adults have disability insurance.

You and your spouse need enough coverage to maintain 60 to 70 percent of your current family income if either of you becomes disabled. Group coverage through your employer is cheapest. If that's not available, try to get a group rate through a group to which you belong.

The older you are when you apply for disability insurance, the higher the cost. You can lower costs by stretching the elimination period. A policy that starts payments on Day 90 of disability will cost 40 percent less than one that pays on Day 30.

DON'T BE AFRAID TO SWITCH

As we have just discussed, the new forms of life insurance which have come on the market in recent years—variable life policies, for example, are much more favorable investments than the older whole life policies. So if you hold such policies, it is not unwise to consider switching. After all, paying into such an excessively costly program over many, many years is a poor way of investing your savings and investment money.

However, there are legal and other restrictions involved in making such a transfer, and these vary from state to state. Consultation with an ethical insurance agent who will give you honest and reasonably impartial advice can help you in determining whether making such a switch is feasible and can be to your advantage.

That's the story on establishing a sound financial base for your family. With an adequate "working fund" and a sound insurance program you are taking a big first step toward long range financial security.

SECOND PHASE: STARTING A SAVINGS PROGRAM

The purpose of starting a savings and investment

program is to provide financial security as the years go by—and particularly in retirement. As we emphasized previously, the fact of inflation makes this a particularly difficult purpose to achieve.

BUILDING A RETIREMENT FUND

Let's look at two examples of how a retirement fund can build over the years through the magic of compound interest. You will note that in addition to the regular contributions to the plans—all earnings are also re-invested as the years roll along.

	Number of years	Amount Each year	Total invested	Total Investing plus Earnings
Example A 6% Compound Interest	1-5	$1,000	$5,000	$5,975.33
	6-10	2,000	15,000	19,946.97
	11-15	3,000	30,000	44,619.02
	16-20	3,000	45,000	77,635.50
	21-25	3,000	60,000	121,819.75
Example B 9% Compound Interest	1-5	$1,000	$5,000	$6,523.33
	6-10	2,000	15,000	22,000.81
	11-15	3,000	30,000	53,421.73
	16-20	3,000	45,000	101,765.96
	21-25	3,000	60,000	172,585.22

Looking at these two examples you can see that even a relatively modest amount of monthly savings grows into a substantial fund that can provide added income in your retirement years. The example also shows that even a few added points of interest on your investments (6% to 9%) very substantially increases the growth of such a fund.

In considering these examples, you must remember, however, that the results shown do not reflect the effect of any income tax requirements, a factor which would severely effect the growth in appreciation shown. This calls attention to the

HOW LONG WILL YOUR MONEY LAST? This chart shows you how long your capital last if your withdraw a fixed amount each year. A * means it will last indefinitely at that rate.						
Percentage of capital withdrawn yearly	**Years money will last if invested at these rates:**					
	5%	6%	7%	8%	9%	10%
8%	21	24	31	*	*	*
10%	15	16	18	21	27	*
12%	11	12	13	15	17	19
14%	10	10	11	12	12	14
16%	8	9	9	10	10	11
18%	7	7	8	8	9	9
20%	6	7	7	7	7	8

YOUR COMPANY'S RETIREMENT PROGRAM: FACTORS TO CONSIDER

● **First**, study the company retirement brochure carefully to be sure you understand all the benefits available to you. Study the details, too, so you know the key rights and restrictions pertaining to each of these benefits. For example, there probably will be restrictions or penalties for withdrawal from the fund. On the other hand, you may be able to borrow against your investments in an emergency and avoid such penalties.

● **Second**, consider the savings funds you have available monthly and carefully select the type of investments you prefer. Perhaps you start with participation in the contributory phase of the pension plan, an approach which earns good returns and helps insure that your basic "pension" at retirement is ample for your needs. Any additional funds available you might put in the stock investment plan. A word of advice here is to study carefully the alternatives available such as the stock of the company itself as well as the several types of mutual funds that also may be included. Then select the one that you feel will earn you the best return with reasonable security over the years.

● **Third**, be sure to include in your planning the objective of reviewing the selections in your company retirement account periodically. You are usually free to make some adjustments in the program as you go along. For example: move some portion of your stock program to a mutual stock or bond fund as a means of providing more safety and diversification. Again times change, and the assignments of funds in your company savings program probably should change occasionally to meet these new circumstances.

---

value of an investment approach that takes advantage of any tax-free or tax-deferred investment program available that year.

The point is, then, that every person or family should have some type of savings or investment program. It may involve only a modest contribution; but these contributions are made consistently into a carefully selected tax-efficient investment that provides a decent return and appreciation.

Now, when you talk about setting up a savings and investment program, you discover people fall into two categories:

● Either they work for a business or other type of organization, or

● They are self-employed.

Let's consider the investment approach appropriate to each of these groups separately.

IF YOU WORK FOR A BUSINESS ORGANIZATION ...

... there are two approaches you can use to make your "beginning" savings and investment program tax-efficient:

● Participation in your company retirement program.

● Use of an Individual Retirement Account (IRA).

YOUR COMPANY'S RETIREMENT PROGRAM

Such company programs vary widely, but a typical program might very well include:

Life, accident and disability insurance, a non-contributory and contributory pension plan, a company savings and stock investment plan and more.

The advantage of such company programs are numerous including the fact they provide the tax-efficient approach that is so important to decent growth in your investment savings. This applies to both the Simplified Employee Pension (SEP) and to the so-called 401 (K) plans. In some instances your initial contributions to these plans are excluded from your earnings before income taxes are withheld. Usually earnings on all types of contributions are sheltered from income taxes while they are held in the plan and until they are withdrawn.

In addition to the tax advantages of such a plan, company contributions often make the plans doubly attractive. The company usually covers many of the required program costs: the non-contributory part of the pension plan, the full cost of some phases of the insurance program, a sizeable percentage add-on for every dollar saved and invested by an employee participant (half a dollar or more in many instances). Just think:

A modest $200 monthly contribution to the company stock program may qualify for up to $100 or more matching contribution by the company for a total of $300 monthly—or $3,600 per year.

Because of the advantages of your company program, you should make every effort to participate using the funds set aside in your budget for such a program.

THE INDIVIDUAL RETIREMENT ACCOUNT

As mentioned earlier, you may also be eligible to set up an IRA. This is a personal savings plan that lets you set aside money for retirement purposes. Contributions to the plan may be tax deductible in whole or in part depending on your circumstances. Earnings on your IRA are not taxed until they are distributed to you. The tax deduction you can take depends on:

1. Whether you are covered by an employer retirement program.
2. If covered, how much income you have.

Even if, because of circumstances, you no longer deduct all or part of the contributions you make to your IRA, you may continue to make non-deductible contributions up to the stipulated yearly limit. These accumulations, along with the deductible ones, will continue to earn income in a tax-free basis until they are withdrawn.

Probably if your employer does not have a retirement program, you will want to make an IRA your first choice for the investment of your retirement savings. Even if you do have a company program, you probably will want to participate to the extent possible under the terms of the of the IRA plan—if you have the funds to do so.

Any of several different investments (including certain gold and silver coins) can be used for an IRA account. In setting up and participating in such a program, you will as always want to do your "homework" and base your decision on sound research and good judgment. Also, since this is the start of your savings and investment plan, you will probably want to be conservative in approach to these investments (as discussed further in the following review of the Keogh accounts for self-employed persons).

IF YOU ARE SELF-EMPLOYED ...

You can take advantage of the tax-efficient benefits of what is called a Keogh plan. This plan is similar to an IRA but is designed specifically for persons who work for themselves: doctors, dentists, store owners, accountants, free lance writers, etc. Only sole proprietors and partners may set up a Keogh plan. Also the plan must meet certain legal requirements.

A tax deduction for contributions to a retirement plan and deferral of tax on income to the plan are benefits that apply to all self-employed persons (including owner-employees) who have a Keogh plan. The amount eligible for deduction is substantial but the formula varies with the specific type of Keogh plan involved.

As mentioned under the discussion of IRA's, you probably—at the start—will want to take a conservative approach to your investments in a Keogh plan. Here are several types of investments you may want to consider both because they provide reasonable safety and security, and because they usually provide an improved rate of earnings over savings accounts.

Certificates of Deposit. These certificates of deposit provide insured security of principal (if they meet legal requirements). They also provide interest earnings at fixed or variable rates that are higher than that earned on savings accounts. The term of the certificate (six months, one year, five years, etc.) usually effects the amount of interest earned.

Certificates of deposit are not strictly liquid investments because of restrictions on withdrawals. But a portion of the funds invested can be made available at regular intervals by staggering maturity dates.

Bonds and Bond Funds. You can buy and sell individual bonds, but many investors find it less complicated to use mutual bond funds in their investment programs. These funds spread their

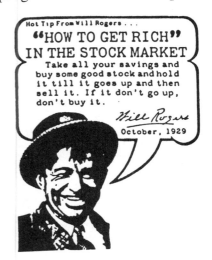

Hot Tip From Will Rogers . . .
"HOW TO GET RICH" IN THE STOCK MARKET
Take all your savings and buy some good stock and hold it till it goes up and then sell it. If it don't go up, don't buy it.

Will Rogers
October, 1929

investments over the bonds of many different companies and governmental organizations, thus providing the security that comes with such diversification.

Bond funds usually are categorized into three groups: corporate, government, and tax-free municipals. Overall they are considered to be relatively low-risk investments, but they do not have guaranteed security in some cases.

Bond funds usually provide an attractive rate of return on your investment. However, the share value of bonds and bond funds, including government bond funds, fluctuate with interest rates: share value goes down when interest rates go up; and share values go up when interest rates go down.

Balanced Mutual Stock Funds and Growth and Income Funds. These funds seek both capital growth and dividend income through balanced investments in both stocks and bonds. They are not as risk free as certificates of deposit or bond funds, but on the average generally provide a good return on your investments over a period of time.

Whatever the type of investment you decide to use in your Keogh plan, you will want to emphasize certain approaches in carrying out your program.

● Select the actual funds and sources in which you plan to invest very carefully. That is, "comparison shop."

● Make your yearly contribution to the plan as large as possible considering the funds you have available and the stipulated limit the Internal Revenue Service permits you to contribute.

● Make your contribution procedure as painless as possible by setting it up so it is handled automatically as a payroll deduction or as an automatic payment from your bank savings account.

IN CONCLUSION...

Let's review the key factors involved in starting an investment program:

● Recognize fully the importance of using tax-efficient approaches for your savings and investment programs.

● Get something started right now so your investment program will have a chance to grow through the effects of consistent contributions and the compounding of interest achieved by reinvesting all earnings as the years go by.

THIRD PHASE: A "FULL-BLOWN" SAVINGS & INVESTMENT PROGRAM

The purpose of this phase of your investment planning is to increase your savings to the point that they will provide for the additional needs and preferences of the family: advanced education for the children, a better home, the possibility of travel now and in retirement.

Your personal situation at this point hopefully is that your income from work has improved—or perhaps your spouse has gone to work as well. You continue to live on your budget (somewhat modified, of course) so funds are not being thoughtlessly wasted. Now you must look beyond the basic start you have made in your employer retirement program, IRA or Keogh plan to a more extensive form of investment.

A SOUND INVESTMENT PROGRAM

In approaching your expanded program, you will continue to look for opportunities to reduce the "bite" of taxation by using the tax-efficient approach where possible.

There are other important factors to look for, too:

Prime quality investments. Whether it is a stock fund, a certificate of deposit, a house or whatever, explore the various alternatives carefully. Comparison shop.

A diversified portfolio. Nobody—even the very best financial planner—is smart enough to call all the "shots" right all the time. Experts agree on one thing: the best way to cut your investment risks is to diversify.

A balanced portfolio. Look for greater potential growth of your investment dollars by including a balance of aggressive, conservative and liquid investment instruments in your portfolio.

Minimum administrative costs. "Loads," fees and commissions can cut your investment profits excessively. So, look for "no load," minimum cost investments and avoid "turning over" your investments more often than necessary.

Consistency of contributions. As we saw earlier, consistency is an important factor in building a substantial investment fund over the years. This approach has the added advantage of letting you "dollar average" your purchases, a process that tends to hold down the average cost of shares which continually fluctuate in price.

STAY TUNED TO THE ECONOMIC CLIMATE

We are not suggesting you should attempt to foresee and react to every change and vagary of the economic situation. But whether the economic forecast appears to be good or bad for the long run, it should be given major consideration in your investment planning.

As to the way to go in applying these investment principles, there are in general two different approaches to take:
- You can do it yourself.
- You can use a financial planner.

THE DO-IT-YOURSELF APPROACH

The points brought out in this discussion will be helpful even if you decide to work with a financial planner at this stage of your investment efforts.

The first step is to do some further study of the investment business generally. Do some reading in the field. Your library is packed with books and periodicals providing sage advice on the subject of investment practices. Take out a subscription to one of the major investment-type publications. It will keep you advised of happenings and prospects in the market. Take one or two courses on the subject of investing at one of your local colleges. At this point you should be ready to go ahead.

We will assume that you have decided to use the mutual fund approach to your investment efforts—an approach you may have already tried in setting up your IRA or Keogh account. This makes sense because, when you do so, you get the diversification you want for safety of your investments plus the professional management and advice of some of the top experts in the field.

Selecting a "family" of funds with a proven track record is the place to start here. Such families include in their offerings a wide variety of mutual stock and bond funds. One big advantage of working with a "family" is that you get the privilege of moving your investments from one type of fund to another quite freely and often without a special charge for the transaction. This is an important, cost-saving factor when you need to switch from more aggressive funds to more conservative ones because of a change in the economic climate.

Getting the background information you want on these fund families is not difficult. Just look through a current investment periodical. Find the names and the toll-free phone numbers of the most prominent families and call them. Ask them to send you information brochures on their funds including details on the performance of their funds.

After you receive this literature, do a thorough "comparison check" of the various families you are considering. Also check the performance record of these funds as shown in frequent research studies, published regularly in the popular financial monthlies. Then and only then make a selection of a family to work with.

BALANCING YOUR PORTFOLIO

Selecting the balance you want in your portfolio is another step. In approaching this matter you should first consider your own personal attitudes toward investment "risk." If you invest in stocks and bonds, you are going to have to face the prospect of market "downs" as well as market "ups." The fact is however, that you can not avoid all risks just by investing conservatively. As an example, a guaranteed savings account will only earn you about 2% on your savings, and inflation in 1993 was approximately 3%.

Also we should mention here the several additional types of mutual funds that should be given consideration at this stage of your planning. Previously we described money market funds, certificates of deposit, bonds and bond funds, and balanced funds. There are also:

Financial Planning

Aggressive Growth and Long Term Growth Funds. These mutual stock funds aim at maximum growth in stock value and capital gains while also providing dividend income, but involve substantial risks because their aggressive investment policy, and their share prices may fluctuate widely.

Index Trust. The difficulty of beating the Dow and other market averages has been shown by numerous studies. So the index trust or index mutual stock fund was created. The list of stocks held by such funds is set up to match those included in one of the popular stock indexes (for example, the Standard and Poor Index). As a result the share price of the index trust closely follows the downs and ups of the market. Since the overall trend of stock market prices over the long run has been up, this characteristic should be advantageous in the long run.

With these points covered, we can go ahead. The purpose of your "balancing" plan is to set up a portfolio of stocks that will give you to some extent the growth potential of aggressive mutual stock funds while retaining a measure of security against market downturns. This is accomplished through the investment of a portion of your savings in aggressive funds, a portion in conservative funds and liquid investments.

The major fund families promote this approach to investment planning, and you will find in their brochure recommendations you can refer to in developing your own basic plan. The following chart also may be helpful. It is a rough summary of the recommendations of a selected group of financial planners as published recently.

You can see that the planners' recommendations became more and more weighted toward conservative investments as the investors get older and the need for security of savings becomes greater. Of course, the long term health of the economy as forecast by the financial community should also be given serious consideration.

TAKING ACTION

Actually setting up your investment program is the final action to take in getting started. Review the stocks available from the family of funds you intend to work with and make a tentative selection of the ones in which you intend to invest—based on their record of performance. Then contact the fund family, and discuss your plans for "balancing" your investment program, the tentative fund selections you have made, and get the counsel of the fund representative.

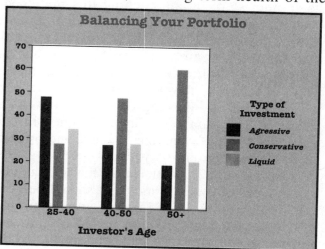

Balancing Your Portfolio

Type of Investment

- Aggressive
- Conservative
- Liquid

Investor's Age

SAVE

1. Take advantage of your employees' pension plan, payroll deduction plan, 401 (K) salary deduction plan, deferred compensation plan.

2. Have a separate savings account.

3. Do not spend your next raise. Keep living at your present level and put the extra money aside.

4. If you get a tax refund or a bonus check, save it.

5. Pay off your mortgage sooner by taking a 15-year loan, paying on a biweekly basis or making extra payments on the principal. This will reduce your total interest costs and build your equity faster.

6. Pay off credit cards so you can save the money you now spend on interest charges.

7. Ask to have all dividends from mutual funds or stocks automatically reinvested.

8. Contribute to an Individual Retirement Account even if you no longer qualify for a full tax deduction on the money you put in. The earnings will still be tax-deferred until retirement.

9. Saving early is a painless way of saving more. Thanks to compounding, $1,000 saved this year will have far greater value when you retire than the same $1,000 put away 10 or 20 years from now.

10. Trim your spending.

IN CONCLUSION ...

... Let's look at the major points we have made leading to a sound and profitable savings and investment program:

First, we emphasized the need for establishing a sound financial base:

- An adequate working fund whose purpose was to provide money for day-to-day living and help minimize costly credit card and other debt.
- An efficient "life insurance" plan that provides adequate protection and coverage at a competitive cost—particularly during the early family years.

Second, we called attention to the need for starting a beginning savings and investment program as early in your career as possible recognizing that:

- Consistent contributions of even modest amounts to such a program build up to significant levels over the years because of the magical effect of "compound interest."
- The use of employer retirement programs, IRA's and Keogh accounts for such initial investments helps to keep them as tax-free as possible and thus helps maximize their growth and appreciation.

If you have gone just this far in your financial planning, you have taken a giant step toward future financial security.

Third, we covered the factors involved in the development of a "full blown" investment program, pointing out that it should:

- Be based on a thorough understanding of the characteristics of a sound program of this type (for example: need for diversification, balance, etc.).
- Involve thoughtful application of these principles whether you "do it yourself" through a mutual fund or with a reliable financial planner.

A FINANCIAL PLANNING CHECKLIST

How prepared are you? have you...

1. Put all your vital financial papers in one place; told someone else where they are; made copies of them?
   Yes ☐ No ☐

2. Figures your retirement expenses, keeping inflation in mind; identified financial assets and projected their growth between now and retirement
   Yes ☐ No ☐

3. Talked over retirement finances with your spouse or, if you are single, with someone close to you?
   Yes ☐ No ☐

4. Figured what survivor's benefits you or your spouse (or other person) would receive if either one of you died? Yes ☐ No ☐

5. Obtained investment and savings information; planned for improving your approach to savings and investments(s) for further investigation?
   Yes ☐ No ☐

If you have circled any NO's—you know where you need to do some work.

WORK SHEET FOR COMPUTING YOUR CASH FLOW

Date:_____

INCOME	LAST YEAR	IN RETIREMENT
Husband's wages or salary	$_____	$_____
Wife's wages or salary	$_____	$_____
Dividends and interest	$_____	$_____
Child support/alimony	$_____	$_____
Annuities, pensions, Social Security	$_____	$_____
Rents, royalties, fees	$_____	$_____
Other_____	$_____	$_____
TOTAL INCOME	$_____	$_____

TAXES		
Income taxes	$_____	$_____
Social Security contributions	$_____	$_____
Property taxes	$_____	$_____
TOTAL TAXES	$_____	$_____

LIVING EXPENSES		
Rent or mortgage payments	$_____	$_____
Food	$_____	$_____
Clothing	$_____	$_____
Utilities	$_____	$_____
Meals out	$_____	$_____
Furniture and other durable goods	$_____	$_____
Recreation, entertainment, vacations	$_____	$_____
Gasoline	$_____	$_____
Car payments	$_____	$_____
Financial and legal services	$_____	$_____
Doctor bills	$_____	$_____
Interest	$_____	$_____
Household maintenance	$_____	$_____
Car repairs	$_____	$_____
Tuition/day care	$_____	$_____
Life and disability insurance premiums	$_____	$_____
Grooming (i.e. laundry, cleaning)	$_____	$_____
Medications	$_____	$_____
Auto insurance premiums	$_____	$_____
Health insurance premiums	$_____	$_____
Other (i.e. gifts) _____	$_____	$_____
TOTAL ANNUAL LIVING EXPENSES	$_____	$_____
Funds available for savings and investments	$_____	$_____

(total income minus taxes and living expenses)

WORK SHEET FOR COMPUTING YOUR NET WORTH

Date: _____

ASSETS

Money in checking account...$ _____

Money in savings account ....$ _____

IRAs, certificates of deposit, other time deposits.............................$ _____

Series E, other government bonds ....$ _____

Stocks or mutual fund certificates ....$ _____

Bond certificates...$ _____

Cash value of life insurance...$ _____

Equity in a vested pension fund...$ _____

Market value of automobiles, other motor vehicles ....$ _____

Household furniture and appliances (keep room-by-room
    inventory separately for insurance) ....$ _____

Jewelry...$ _____

Sports and musical equipment..$ _____

Antiques and collections (keep separate inventory).........................$ _____

Clothing (particularly fur coats and other big-price tag items) ....$ _____

Loans receivable ....$ _____

Cash value of any business you might have ....$ _____

Other assets..$ _____

    TOTAL ASSETS...$ _____

LIABILITIES

Mortgage on home or other real estate ....$ _____

Unpaid taxes ....$ _____

Notes (total unpaid, not current amount due) ....$ _____

Installment debts (see below[*])..$ _____

Charge account debts (see below[*])...$ _____

Other personal obligations (think hard)...$ _____

    TOTAL LIABILITIES...$ _____

    YOUR NET WORTH[**] ....$ _____

KEEP A CURRENT LIST OF ALL ACCOUNT NUMBERS

[*] Amounts due (not monthly installments but total balances) in accounts with credit card and gasoline companies, department stores and other retailers, and to anyone else to whom you owe money. This is an important total to know and to review periodically; many who run into credit problems do so because they have lost track of how much they owe overall—it's too easy to charge.

[**] To compute your net worth, take a total of your liabilities and deduct the amount from your total assets (if the amount is larger, you're facing trouble). The result is your net worth. After you've done this one, subsequent surveys will be easier; you will have basic figures that will only need reviewing and adjusting. A 20% increase in net worth annually is considered ideal—but don't really expect such a gain until later years.

SOCIAL SECURITY

Social Security is America's most important financial program. Millions count on it for their survival. In fact, some 36 million checks go out each month. Social Security is essentially a family program that offers these major benefits:

1. Disability Benefits
2. Survivor Benefits
3. Retirement Benefits
4. Medicare Benefits

Benefits can also be paid to dependents of retired, disabled, or deceased workers (refer to the Dependent Benefits Chart). Each of the major benefits will be discussed in more detail later. As you can see, Social Security acts as a kind of insurance that will play a role in your family's life at important junctures: retirement, disability, and death.

BECOMING INSURED

For any benefits to be paid, the worker must have worked long enough and sometimes recent enough to qualify. Work performed under Social Security earns "quarters of coverage" (referred to from now on as credits). Four credits can be earned in a calendar year. In years before 1978, a worker had to actually earn $50 or more during a calendar quarter to get a credit. Beginning in 1978, yearly credits are determined by dividing the total covered earnings by a yearly increment. These increments increase every year. In 1995 one credit is earned for each $630; therefore, $2,520 will earn the four credit maximum.

The number of credits needed depends on the type of benefit involved. As a "rule of thumb," one credit is needed for each year that elapses after age 22 up to the year of age 62, death, or disability. It does not matter when the credits are earned. Disability benefits require the worker to not only be "fully insured" but also have recent work. Some survivor benefits can be paid if the worker is not "fully insured," but has earned credits in six of the thirteen calendar quarters prior to death. By doing so the worker is considered to be "currently insured." This is especially helpful when very young workers die and leave dependent children and young widows/widowers or former widows/widowers caring for those children.

YOU'LL NEED 60-75% OF YOUR PRESENT INCOME TO MAINTAIN YOUR PRESENT LIVING STANDARD IN RETIREMENT.

Some people think that their Social Security benefits will be based on the number of credits they have. This is not true. The dollar amount of any benefits paid has nothing to do with the number of credits you have. You either qualify or not qualify for benefits based on credits. The calculation of the benefit amount will be discussed later.

THINGS TO DO EVEN IF RETIREMENT IS A LONG WAY OFF

The Social Security Administration has been keeping records of your earnings throughout your working life. But are those records accurate and up-to-date? Nothing could be worse than filing for your benefits and finding yourself short-changed or delayed because of errors that happened in the distant past.

Check Your Record: A service offered by the Social Security Administration gives workers who request it a printout of their credited earnings as well as an estimate of the dollar amount of Social Security monthly benefits they can expect in the event of disability or retirement and an estimate of the dollar amount of any survivor benefits payable. Use the envelope in this book to request your personal earnings and benefit statement. Mail the envelope to the Social Security Data Operations Center, P.O. Box 7004, Wilkes Barre, PA 18767-7004. When your printout is received, review it carefully and report any errors immediately to the social security office nearest you. You can do this by telephone. It probably would not hurt to note the date, time, and name of the person you spoke with in your own records.

Check for Overpayments: You may also find an employer did not stop collecting Social Security taxes after reaching the maximum taxable amount in a given year. In this event you can receive a refund or a credit against your federal income tax. All you have to do is request it on your income tax return.

RETIREMENT BENEFITS

Very few people find their Social Security checks enough to cover their expenses. READY OR NOT suggests you take a look at what you can expect from Social Security and how it will fit into your retirement plans. Your Social Security retirement benefits will be based on your lifetime earnings. Many people think that only the last five years are used to calculate benefits. Nothing could be further from the truth. Almost all people retiring in the future (born in 1929 and later) will have 35 years of earnings averaged together and used in their benefit computation.

If you would like a more detailed explanation of how your retirement benefit is figured, ask Social Security for a copy of the fact sheet, "How Your Retirement Benefit is Figured." As noted earlier, Social Security will also provide you an estimate of your expected monthly retirement benefits along with a printout of your yearly earnings, if you write the Operations Center in Wilkes Barre.

EARLY RETIREMENT VS. LATE RETIREMENT

As you look ahead to retirement, you may be thinking "… the earlier the better." But if Social Security is going to be your only source of income, "the later, the better" applies.

Early retirement decreases your retirement benefits. Currently, if you retire at age 62 (the earliest age), you would receive only 80% of the amount collectible at age 65. However, in terms of dollars received from Social Security, a worker retiring at 65 will have to live to age 77 to equal the total dollars received by a worker who retired at age 62.

If you decide to retire before age 65, or you have very low earnings, you should consider filing early. For a more detailed explanation of the best time to contact Social Security to avoid possible loss of benefits, refer to the section entitled, "When to Contact Social Security."

Age to Receive Full Social Security Benefits

Year of Birth	Full Retirement Age
1937 or earlier	65
1938	65 and 2 months
1939	65 and 4 months
1940	65 and 6 months
1941	65 and 8 months
1942	65 and 10 months
1943-1954	66
1955	66 and 2 months
1956	66 and 4 months
1957	66 and 6 months
1958	66 and 8 months
1959	66 and 10 months
1960 and later	67

* If you take monthly benefits before full retirement age, your benefits are reduced.

If you wait to retire after age 65, your benefit is increased an extra 3% for each year you continue working after age 65 (delayed retirement credits). The percentage of these delayed credits increases over the next 25 years to reach 8% by the year 2009.

As a quick check on how much you can look forward to at full retirement age, consider what percentage of your income will be replaced by your retirement benefits. If your lifetime earnings were average, you can expect to receive a benefit of about $10,296 a year. The average eligible couple receives about $15,444 a year (both worker and spouse at full retirement age).

If you have always paid the maximum in Social Security deductions, you can count on a benefit of about 24% of that amount. In 1994 the maximum earnings subject to Social Security taxes was $60,600. That gives you approximately $14,400 a year in retirement benefits.

SPECIAL NOTE: Even if you file for reduced benefits, at age 65 you will be given credit for any months you did not receive a full check because of work. This is commonly referred to by Social Security as an automatic adjustment of your reduction factor.

WHAT YOU PAY FOR SOCIAL SECURITY
(Worker Amount Matched by Employer)

Year	% Tax Rate	Maximum Taxable Wage Base	Employee Maximum Tax
1950	1.50%	$ 3,000	$ 45.00
1960	3.00	4,800	144.00
1970	4.80	7,800	374.40
1980	6.13	25,900	1,587.67
1990	7.65	51,000	3,924.45
1992	7.65	55,500	4,245.75
1993	7.65	57,600	4,406.40
1994	7.65	60,600	4,635.90
1995	7.65	61,200	4,681.80

Amount for each year is based on increases in average earnings of all employees in the country.

HUSBANDS AND WIVES

Both husband and wife are eligible to receive Social Security benefits even if only one has earned enough credits. The worker that qualifies will receive at retirement his or her own benefits. The "non-qualified" spouse (the spouse who has not worked enough to qualify) will receive a benefit equal to a percentage of the worker's benefit. Usually the "non-qualified" spouse must be age 62 to receive this spousal benefit.

If both husband and wife qualify on their own for Social Security, both will receive their own benefits. In those instances where one spouse's benefit is less than half of the other's, the lesser-paid spouse will usually receive his or her own benefit *plus* a spousal benefit.

The spousal benefit provisions in no way reduce the worker's benefits. Similarly, spousal benefits payable to the current spouse are not affected by any benefits being paid to a former spouse.

One important issue to note here is that while a spouse may be eligible at age 62 for benefits without having worked, the same is not true for disability benefits. You must have worked and meet certain other conditions to receive disability benefits.

This chapter on Social Security has been prepared with the helpful assistance of Jim Caulder, a Social Security specialist with the firm, Informed Decisions, of Columbia, South Carolina

A WORD ABOUT THE FOLLOWING SOCIAL SECURITY TABLES

Remember that the maximum amount of earning covered by Social Security was lower in past year than it is now. Those years of lower limits must b counted in with the higher ones of recent years t figure your average earnings and thus the amour of your monthly retirement check.

The Social Security tables are based on assump tions for people age 65 at the start of 1995 wh earned the salaries shown in 1994—assuming the had worked steadily in covered employment sinc age 22.

Except for persons who have always paid th maximum, the amount payable in any particula case could stray well beyond those illustrated.

In fact, if a person spent much of their career either in non-covered employment or outside th work force altogether, their payment might be les than the lowest shown even though they are nov earning considerably more than $10,000.

The tables also assume that the worker does nc qualify for a "non covered" pension.

Anyone who does qualify for a pension base on work that was not covered for Social Securit taxes may not have the same computation methoc Social Security can provide you with a fact shee entitled "A Pension From Work Not Covered B Social Security" that explains in detail a modifie computation.

	[1] Salary in Year Before Retirement	[2] Monthly	[3] First Year Social Security Income	[4] Approximate Replacement Ratio

Estimated Monthly and First-Year Social Security Income Payable as of January 1995 to a 65-year-old Person

Salary in Year Before Retirement	Monthly	First Year Social Security Income	Approximate Replacement Ratio
$10,000	$459	$5,508	54%
15,000	589	7,068	46%
20,000	720	8,640	42%
25,000	838	10,056	38%
30,000	881	10,572	33%
35,000	906	10,872	29%
40,000	926	11,112	26%
45,000	941	11,292	24%
55,500	1,128	13,536	24%
60,600	1,200	14,400	24%

Because $60,600 is the maximum taxable 1994 Social Security wage base, Social Security will, of course, replace an increasingly smaller portion of earnings that exceed it.

Maximum 1995 income for beneficiaries stated. Maximum benefits for a worker retiring in 1995 is $1,200 per month—an increase of $53 per month over 1994. Replacement rate numbers are only tentative until prior year average wages are determined.

These figures assume you have worked regularly and received yearly wage increases. Mail the envelope accompanying this book to Social Security for a more precise estimate of your benefits.

SURVIVOR BENEFITS

Remember that survivor benefits to dependent children and young widows/widowers can be paid based on "fully or currently" insured status. The amount of benefits payable to any survivor is determined by the covered earnings of the deceased worker.

A rate is calculated as if the worker had become age 62 in the year of death and a primary insurance amount (PIA) is established. Each dependent is entitled to a percentage of the PIA; however, there is a maximum amount payable. (Refer to the Dependent's Benefits Chart for more specific information.)

A one-time lump-sum death payment of $255 is payable to either a widow/widower entitled to benefits, a widow or widower not entitled to monthly benefits, or to children entitled to benefits.

Benefits due divorced spouses are not considered in the family maximum. In other words, the divorced spouse takes nothing away from the current spouse or widow and vice versa.

Automatic Social Security Cost-of-Living Adjustments

Once you are on the Social Security benefit rolls, your checks will increase automatically to keep pace with increases in the cost of living.

In addition, additional earnings after initial entitlement can be considered in a recalculation of your rate.

DISABILITY BENEFITS

The risk of disability hangs over all of us. A loss of earnings due to a severe injury or illness can affect a family more than the retirement or even death of the breadwinner.

Social Security provides basic protection against disability for most Americans and their families. Currently about 3.2 million adults from all walks of life receive disability checks. There is a full five-month waiting period before disability payments can begin. This period begins with the first full month of disability and ends five months later. No payment is made for that period.

As mentioned earlier, a disabled worker must be fully insured and have recent work under Social Security in order to be qualified. During the ten-year period just before becoming disabled, the worker must have five years of credits (20). **Workers becoming disabled prior to age 31 need fewer credits.** And workers who are blind must only be "fully insured." It is very important for a worker to understand the "recent work" requirement, particularly persons opting for "early out" retirements with their company. If you plan on retiring prior to age 56 you should consider working at another job and acquiring four credits per year through the year you attain age 56. By doing so, you will continue to have enough recent work to qualify you for disability until you reach age 62.

Dependents of disabled workers can also receive benefits within the family maximum payable. (Refer to the Benefits for Dependents Chart).

OTHER RESOURCES

Social Security publishes many pamphlets and brochures about the various programs it administers. Listed below is an alphabetical list of current Social Security fact sheets available from the Social Security Administration. You can call toll-free 1-800-772-1213 to request any copies you might want.

A Pension From Work Not Covered by Social Security
Agricultural Workers
Farm Rental Income
Financing Social Security
Government Pension Offset
Help For Low Income Medicare Beneficiaries
Household Workers
How to File an Unfair Treatment Complaint
How Work Affects Your Social Security Benefits
How Your Retirement Benefit is Figured
Military Service and Social Security
Reviewing Your Disability
Social Security and Your Right to Representation
Special Wage Payments After Retirement
The Appeals Process

3 WAYS TO INSURE A SOUND FINANCIAL RETIREMENT

BILL KRESSE

Social Security Benefits for Dependents

Dependent is age...	and...	then these benefits may be payable...	at the following % of PIA...
0-19	a child of a deceased or entitled worker	minor child or student benefits	50% (worker alive) 75% (worker deceased)
18 and older	disabled before age 22 and parent is either deceased or entitled	disabled adult child benefits	50% (worker alive) 75% (worker deceased)
up to age 65	a young widow(er) or divorced widow(er) with child in care under age 16	mother/father benefits	75%
50-60	a disabled widow(er) or a surviving divorced widow(er)	disabled widow(er) benefits	71.5%
60+	a widow(er), surviving divorced spouse	widow(er)'s benefit	varies from 71.5% to 100% depending age at entitlement
62+	1) currently married to entitled worker	spouse benefits	50%
	2) divorces after 10 years of marriage to entitled worker	divorced spouse benefits	50%
	3) divorced after 10 years of marriage to an age 62 worker not entitled but insured	independently entitled divorced spouse benefits	50%
	4) surviving parent	parent's benefits	82.5% if one 75% each if two

MEDICARE BENEFITS

Medicare is a national health insurance program for people age 65. It is administered by the Social Security Administration.

Whether or not you apply for Social Security at age 65, you should apply at least three months in advance of your 65th birthday to be covered by Medicare.

Details of Medicare are spelled out in the Health Insurance chapter (see pages 54-55).

WORKING AND RECEIVING SOCIAL SECURITY

With the exception of a disabled worker or an adult disabled child, *all* Social Security beneficiaries are subject to an earnings test up until age 70. Social Security sets a yearly limit on the amount of earnings you can have before withholding some of your benefits. These limits increase every year.

If you are under age 65 in 1995 the limit is $8,160. The limit is $11,280 for persons age 65 and older. There is no limit once you are age 70 and, in fact, earnings during the month you turn 70 and thereafter do not count toward the annual limit. When we speak of earnings we are only talking about income from work or profits from self-employment. Investment income (dividends, real estate, rentals, and return on capital) is not counted. Neither are pensions.

If you do earn more than the yearly limit, you lose some of your Social Security benefits. One dollar is withheld for every two dollars above the limit for all persons younger than age 65. One dollar for every *three* is withheld for persons 65 through 69. This "one for three" rule is significant. Many people could receive some Social Security benefits for the year even while working full time. See the section entitled, "When to Contact Social Security."

There is a special rule that can apply to your initial year of retirement. It is called the "grace year" rule and in effect means that workers are allowed a monthly earning limit for each month in that year. The monthly limit is simply the annual limits divided by twelve. This special rule usually applies only for one year but helps those persons who have high earnings in the months prior to retirement.

For more information, ask Social Security for the fact sheet, "How Work Affects Your Social Security Benefits."

WHEN TO CONTACT SOCIAL SECURITY

Survivors of deceased workers should contact Social Security as soon as possible after the death of the worker. Disabled workers should contact Social Security as soon as their physician advised that their medical condition is expected to last at least twelve months. Persons reaching age 62 should follow the procedures below. Effective with January 1991, retirement applications can no longer be retroactive. Prior to 1991, if there were any advantages in having your retirement claim effective earlier than the month you filed, Social Security would allow the claim to be effective as early as six months before your application date. Since this can no longer be done, **Ready or Not** recommends that persons reaching age 62 should:

A. Contact Social Security three months prior to age 62 if you have retired or are planning to retire at age 62 *OR*
B. Contact Social Security every January (even if working full time). Provide them with an estimate of your current year earnings, and ask them to determine the dollar amount of any benefits you might be eligible for if you filed a formal claim. Remember to tell Social Security if there are any dependents who will also be eligible for benefits on your record.

BENEFITS MAY BE TAXABLE

Up to one-half of your benefits may be subject to the Federal income tax for any year in which your adjusted gross income plus non-taxable interest income and one-half of your Social Security benefits exceeds a base amount of $25,000 for an individual, $32,000 for a couple, and zero for a couple filing separately. Should your adjusted gross income exceed $34,000 for an individual or $44,000 for a couple, 85% of excess benefits are taxable.

SUPPLEMENTAL SECURITY INCOME

People in financial need who are 65 or older or people of any age who are blind or disabled may be eligible for a monthly cash payment from the Federal government. These payments are called supplemental security income (SSI).

People may be eligible for payments if they have little or no regular cash income and don't own much in the way of assets that can be turned into cash. The Social Security Administration operates the program but SSI is not the same as Social Security. Social Security funds are not used to make SSI payments. Applications for SSI are made at the Social Security office. In most states Medicaid is provided for anyone eligible for SSI.

ADDRESS OF SOCIAL SECURITY DATA OPERATIONS CENTER

Social Security Data Operations Center
P.O. Box 7004
Wilkes Barre, PA 18767-7004

PLANNING YOUR ESTATE

If a fire destroys your home, how much will you lose? If you have fire insurance, you may have the value of the house covered to the extent that you can have it replaced for no additional expense. What will happen in the event of your death? Will your estate be turned over to your family without loss? Carelessness in making plans for your estate will increase the chances that what you have carefully accumulated over the years may be disposed of in ways you would not approve.

Before you skip on to the next chapter with the thought that you don't have an estate, and that everything will be left to your spouse, let's take a look at what is an "estate." Maybe you don't have much to leave when you die, but the U.S. government may have a less modest opinion of what you are leaving. The federal government imposes a tax on estates and some states have their own inheritance or estate taxes.

Don't assume that your wife will automatically receive your property. If there is no will, the estate may be disposed of according to the laws of decent of the state where the property is located. Even if you have all your property jointly owned, the absence of a will may cause her to have to wait several months before gaining possession of the property.

OWNING PROPERTY

Check with your attorney as to which of four types of property ownership best suits your needs.
They are:

Joint Tenancy with Right of Survivorship: When two or more people hold property jointly and one person dies—the other or others receive the dead person's interest automatically.

Tenancy by the Entirety: Limited to husbands and wives. Both spouses have to agree as to disposing the property.

Tenancy in Common: When two or more people hold shares in property and one dies, his or her shares passes to that person's heirs.

Community Property: Eight states have laws that hold that all property acquired during marriage is owned by each spouse equally.

RELUCTANCE TO MAKE A WILL

Many individuals reaching retirement age have not made a will. The reasons may be: superstition and procrastination. Some seem to feel that thinking about a will may hasten the moment when it can be needed. If we don't notice approaching age or think about mortality, maybe it won't notice us. Many people do not want to think about such a "grim" subject. "It will be easier to think about it tomorrow!"

"AND ALL MY WORLDLY POSSESSIONS"

An individual's estate consists of the many valuable assets accumulated through a variety of methods during the lifetime. These include: life insurance, accounts in savings banks and savings and loan associations, social security, stocks, bonds, pension and profit-sharing plans, real estate, stock options, inheritances, business and professional interests, investments, employee fringe benefits, etc.

For the purpose of taxation the "gross estate" is composed of all assets an individual owns at the time of death, plus any property at the time of death, and gifts made in contemplation of death. "Taxable estate" is the gross estate, less liabilities.

WHY MAKE A WILL?

A will is a written instrument executed with the formalities prescribed by law, whereby a person directs the disposition of his or her property after death.

If you make a will, your property will go to the persons named and in the amounts you specify. If you fail to make a will, the law arbitrarily distributes your property according to prevailing regulations.

Making a will may save money by reducing expenses. If you do not have a will, your heirs will not be able to sell, distribute, or handle property without the expense of asking a court for authority. If you do not make a will, your estate or inheritance taxes may be higher than they need legally be. If you do not make a will, the person who administers your estate will have to post a bond. If you do not make a will, your property may be dealt with, your business operated or concluded, and your real estate sold with losses.

If you make a will, you can name the person you wish to handle your estate.

DISADVANTAGES OF LEAVING AN ESTATE WITHOUT A WILL

Where no will exists, the matter of who will administer the estate can be the occasion for painful disputes and needless expense. When an executor is named, he must post a bond, the premium for which must be taken from the estate. (A bond can be dispensed with if the will so provides.) This administrator can only liquidate your assets, pay your debts, and distribute the remainder of your property. He has only limited authority to deal with real property, business, or other property.

DISPOSITIONS OF ESTATES

You can use a will to make outright disposition of your assets. You can also make outright gifts of parcels of your estate during your lifetime. You can create a "trust" by transferring your estate or part of it to a trustee. You live off the income it provides during your lifetime, and the principal is disposed of later. You can also set up a "testamentary trust" which assures income for your spouse or dependents. This type of arrangement protects them against their own inexperience in the management of the estate.

KEEPING WILLS UP TO DATE

Wills which were valid years ago may need to be reviewed periodically. Circumstances may have changed so that the things referred to in the will no longer exist, or things exist which the original will did not contemplate.

The following changes should cause you to look again at the condition of your will:

- Change of mind about beneficiaries
- Executor dies
- Change in family situation
- Change in financial situation
- Change in the nature of assets
- Change in the needs of the beneficiaries
- Change of residence, state or country

CONSIDER TRUSTS

Trusts may be an ideal method to handle some of your assets. Basically, a trust is a plan whereby a trustee holds money that you have transferred, and manages it according to your written trust agreement.

Trusts may be living or testamentary; revocable or irrevocable. Say you wished to transfer twenty thousand dollars to a trust for your grandchildren's education while you're alive—a living trust. If the trust was created by your will, it's testamentary.

A revocable trust can be canceled by the person who establishes it; an irrevocable trust cannot be terminated.

Trusts do cost money—check with your attorney or the trust officer of your bank.

Trusts have advantages under certain conditions. They could save money and time. Be informed by reading books and articles on trusts. Check with your library and consult your attorney.

MORE READING

A Consumer's Guide to Probate (D13822) from AARP's Consumer Affairs Section. For a free copy send a postcard to the title and number, AARP Fulfillment, 601 E Street, NW, Washington, DC 20049; allow two to four weeks for delivery.

TO AVOID PROBLEMS LATER YOU'LL NEED:

A Power of Attorney	There may be an occasion when you could not act on your own behalf in certain legal matters. You may grant someone you trust your "Power of Attorney" to act for you. You do this by signing a notarized document specifying the details of what matter the "Power of Attorney" should represent you in and for what period of time the document is effective.
A Durable Power of Attorney for Health Care	A Durable Power of Attorney for Health Care makes clear your wishes about your future medical care. It tells doctors and hospital employees whether you want to be kept alive if you're in a coma or suffering a terminal illness beyond all reasonable hope of recovery. It names someone you trust to carry out your wishes. You can specify what should be done after consultation with family members, medical doctors and your Minister, Priest or Rabbi. State laws differ—check with an attorney or your local Office of Aging.
To Update or Make a Will	There may be changes in your situation, be sure your will reflects your wishes.
To Consider Setting Up a Trust	It avoids probate and allows a trustee to manage your assets if you become incompetent.

LOCATE IMPORTANT PAPERS

KEEP THEM SAFE BUT ACCESSIBLE

LET SOMEONE ELSE KNOW WHERE THEY ARE

WILL FACT SHEET

Telephone Number: _____   _____
                        (Home)   (Date This Form Completed)

_____
(Business)

Address: _____
                    (Home)

_____
(Street)

_____
(City)   (State) (Zip)   (County)

	SELF	SPOUSE
NAME		
SOCIAL SECURITY NUMBER		
OCCUPATION		
DATE AND PLACE OF BIRTH		
DRIVER'S LICENSE NUMBER		
MILITARY SERVICE		
DATE/PLACE OF MARRIAGE		
DATE OF DIVORCE		
DEATH OF SPOUSE		

CHILDREN

1. _____ _____
        Name   Date of Birth

_____
Place of Birth

_____
If married, name of husband or wife

_____
Present address (Street, City, State, Zip)

3. _____ _____
        Name   Date of Birth

_____
Place of Birth

_____
If married, name of husband or wife

_____
Present address (Street, City, State, Zip)

3. _____ _____
        Name   Date of Birth

_____
Place of Birth

_____
If married, name of husband or wife

_____
Present address (Street, City, State, Zip)

4. _____ _____
        Name   Date of Birth

_____
Place of Birth

_____
If married, name of husband or wife

_____
Present address (Street, City, State, Zip)

BENEFIT PLANS

Value, if known

Pension Plan _____ $ _____

Thrift Plan _____   _____

Profit-Sharing Plan _____   _____

Other _____   _____

_____   _____

_____   _____

_____   _____

HEALTH INSURANCE

Company _____   Policy Numbers _____

Names(s) of Insured _____   Beneficiary(ies) _____

Location of Policies _____   Agent _____

_____   Address & Phone _____

_____   _____

Company _____   Policy Numbers _____

Name(s) of Insured _____   Beneficiary(ies) _____

Location of Policies _____   Agent _____

_____   Address & Phone _____

_____   _____

HOME AND AUTO INSURANCE

Company _____   Policy Numbers _____

Type of Coverage _____   Location of Policies _____

Agent _____   _____

Address & Phone _____   _____

_____   _____

Company _____   Policy Numbers _____

Type of Coverage _____   Location of Policies _____

Agent _____   _____

Address & Phone _____   _____

_____   _____

ASSETS INVENTORY

Item	Current Market Value	Original Cost	Location	Ownership
Home				
Business				
Household furniture				
Checking account				
Stamp collection				
Savings account				
Pension plans				
Bonds				
Trust funds				
Stock				

LIABILITY INVENTORY

Loans _____ $ _____

Debts _____ $ _____

Mortgages _____ $ _____

LIFE INSURANCE

Insurance Company Or Agent	Type & No. of Policy	Face Amount of Policy	Cash Surrender Value, if Any	Date of Issue	Present Beneficiary Primary Contingent	Amount of Accidental Death Provision

LOCATION OF
RECORDS, CERTIFICATES, LICENSES

Birth _____   Deed _____

Marriage _____   Mortgage _____

Adoption _____   Title Policy Insurance_____

Citizenship _____   Title Abstract _____

Prenuptial _____   Surveys_____

Postnuptial_____   Insurance Policies _____

Divorce _____   Tax Receipts_____

Discharge papers_____   Leases_____

Building Costs _____

SAFE DEPOSIT BOX

LOCATION _____

BOX NUMBER _____

WHO HAS ACCESS _____

KEYS LOCATED _____

CONTENTS _____

A list of how you would like your personal effects distributed (jewelry, art, etc.) and your burial instructions should be placed in a safe place but *not* in the safe deposit box.

INDIVIDUALS KNOWLEDGEABLE WITH MY AFFAIRS

Attorney _____   Power of Attorney _____

Address _____   Address _____

Telephone _____   Telephone _____

Accountant _____   Banker _____

Address _____   Address _____

Telephone _____   Telephone _____

Broker _____   Clergyman/Rabbi _____

Address _____   Address _____

Telephone _____   Telephone _____

Doctor _____   Employer/Union Rep. _____

Address _____   Address _____

Telephone _____   Telephone _____

Executor of Estate_____   Insurance Agent _____

Address _____   Address _____

Telephone _____   Telephone _____

"A fool and his money …"
"Let the buyer beware."
"There's one born every minute!"

Hanging on to the money you have in retirement is often a difficult task, but by keeping your eyes wide open you can avoid the common pitfalls that threaten to deplete your pocketbook.

THE PURCHASER'S PROFILE

Recent studies indicate that the consumer has buying habits which are designed to needlessly strain his budget. Consider the following:

- Most grocery shoppers never use a list and shop in only one grocery store.
- Customers who charge their purchases buy three times as much as customers who pay cash.
- Many buy nonessential items on credit for which they would not pay cash.
- Customers fail to use appliances and mechanical purchases properly and pay for service calls that could be avoided.
- Many people do not know how to budget their paycheck to last throughout the month.

Some have estimated that as much as 20% of the average grocery bill could be saved if some simple rules were followed in the supermarket. The average family spends about 25% of its budget on food. If your income is $600 a month, your food budget could be $150. A savings of 20% would see you having the same amount of food for $120. How can this be done? We thought you would never ask!

SAVINGS IN THE SUPERMARKET

1. Always plan your shopping for food; use a list.
2. Never shop while hungry.
3. Avoid impulse buying.
4. Shop at two or three different supermarkets for competitive prices.
5. Shop only once or twice a week, and do not stay beyond a half hour. (Each minute you stay after a half-hour costs you 50¢!)
6. Avoid paying for packaging, as may be the case in some convenience foods.
7. Consider buying the local store's brand which corresponds to the quality of nationally advertised brands. You can save up to 20¢ on an item.
8. Avoid diet foods, if possible. Buy regular foods and eat less. (However, if you are on a special diet prescribed by your doctor—salt free, low cholesterol, etc.—you should, of course, stay within what he or she recommends.)
9. Learn to compare costs per unit price. The larger size may be a great deal cheaper.
10. Learn to substitute fish, poultry, smaller quantities of meat for meals which relied heavily on meat. (Rice, noodles, etc. extend the meat dish, as can the use of sauces and gravies.)
11. Become familiar with grading regulations. A higher grade may refer to the appearance of meat, eggs, rather than to nutritional value.
12. Watch weekly specials and buy the items which are reduced, leaving other items to be purchased at a store with most reasonable price.
13. Keep a list of prices charged for similar items in the different stores you shop.
14. Get pre-shopping information from Consumer Report and Consumer Union.
15. Check coupon and trading stamps to see that you are not paying higher prices for items in the store to make up for savings.
16. Make sure that "specials" are items you actually need.
17. Use nonfat dry and evaporated milk and cut a third off your milk bill.
18. Arrive at a sensible balance between your time, your money, and your health.
19. Stock up on items in season and on sale.

CREDIT CARDS
EASY TO GET, EASY TO USE— AND EASY TO ABUSE

It weighs less than half an ounce but it can, if misused, put a crushing burden on those who consider themselves its beneficiaries.

We are referring to credit cards—the basis of today's plastic consumer economy.

Credit cards are now easy to get. Too easy, perhaps. Be careful.

"Pay cash and stay out of trouble. You don't go overboard on things you want but can't really afford."

A general-use credit card carried in wallet or pocketbook can be a safe substitute for money (a check is even better)—if the card is cared for properly. Department store cards also are useful in shopping excursions when handled reasonably.

The words **"when handled reasonably"** are important.

The same thinking should go into a credit card transaction as goes into one involving cash.

Also keep in mind that **when you put a purchase on a card and do not pay for it when the bill comes in, interest charges begin**. What you put on the card costs you more if months drag on. Using cards mean you're using credit at rates that may be as high as 20% (about 1.7% a month). Bargains bought with a card very quickly become no bargain at all. Once again: Be Careful.

CAUTION IN THE CAR LOT

The same care used in making a shopping list for groceries can also help the prospective car owner find satisfaction in his purchase. Your car should be a source of satisfaction to you … in terms of price, appearance and performance. Make the following decisions before you arrive at the car lot:

1. Determine the kind of car you need for the next two years.
2. Decide how much you can afford to spend. This should include all the optionals and cost of financing. Determine the amount of monthly payments you can afford.
   If your car payments are more than half of what you allow for housing, some people feel you are paying too much for the car.
3. Find out how much your present car is worth. Do not accept the word of the car salesman. Some have been known to be unfairly critical of cars submitted for trade-ins!
   Go to your bank and ask for the Kelly Blue Book, the Official Used Car Guide of the National Automobile Dealers Association. It gives the amount your car is worth if it is not over eight years old.
4. Decide what a realistic price will be for the new car. The dealer has about 20-25% profit in the car. Look at the retail price, subtract the transportation costs in getting the car to the dealer, and calculate what margin of profit is built into the car. Many dealers will be satisfied if they can make $500 on a new car.
5. Decide how you will finance the car, if you are one of the 92% of new car buyers who must finance the new car purchase. The bank or a credit union will give better rates than the company related to the car agency.
6. Be alert to techniques used by car salesmen:
   (a) **Highball**—This consists of an exceptionally generous allowance on your old car. Just before the deal is made, the salesman discovers an error and has to offer a lower figure.
   (b) **Lowball**—For the buyer prepared to pay cash, there is a quote of a low purchase price, which must be corrected just before the sale is made.
   (c) **Unauthorized offer**—The salesman

MONEY SAVING TIPS

PAY BY CASH OR CHECK

PAY BILLS EACH MONTH BY DUE DATE

BILLS

KEEP THE NUMBER OF CARDS TO A MINIMUM

makes an attractive offer, and just when you are ready to buy he tries to get the approval of the sales manager … unsuccessfully.

These techniques are designed to create a fever of enthusiasm over owning the new car. When the deal appears about to fall through, it is like taking your car away from you.

Automobile repair is another sad chapter that could be written in the life of the frustrated consumer. Experts estimate that $25 billion is spent NEEDLESSLY each year on car repairs.

Even if you aren't a mechanic, you can: Keep the water and oil clean (check both and change the latter according to the instructions in the owner's manual); keep your battery terminals clean and keep your tires inflated to the pressure recommended in your owner's manual.

Locate a friend you can trust who can help with the maintenance of your car. Use the services of a diagnostic clinic to obtain estimates of anticipated repairs.

Learn something about automobile maintenance and repair. Read books like Anthony Till's *What You Should Know Before You Have Your Car Repaired*, Sherbourne Press, Inc.

USED CAR PURCHASES

A car has depreciated half of its original value after two years, but may still have three-quarters of its life left. The perils which confront the buyer in this field are so numerous that we hesitate to make recommendations. Some people trade cars when they begin to have trouble with them. Some people buy the cars which other people traded when they began to have trouble with them. We would like to help you join the ranks of the first group and avoid running around with members of the second!

Check your Blue Book; determine the kind of car you want to buy; find the most expensive example of the model you want; have it checked out by an independent mechanic; get the car for the best price you can obtain from the dealer. Contacting the former owner may help; checking the maintenance records can't hurt; shopping around for competitive deals might work; doing business with a reputable used car dealer who has been in business for a long time and has established a record for honesty and service may be the best advice yet.

HEALTH CARE HAZARDS

The U.S. government estimates that Americans spend $500 million each year on vitamins, minerals, and health remedies they don't need. The Food and Drug Administration emphasizes that sensible eating can provide most of the nutrients which the body needs, and common foods may have these qualities as well as more expensive foods.

Americans are vulnerable to health swindles because we are health-conscious.

We have come to think of science as achieving all of its goals. It must have found a remedy for our ailment.

We are exposed to articles and advertisements about health.

We hear about new health practices in other countries, often different from those in our own country.

The American Medical Association suggests that you can recognize a "quack" by any of the following traits:
- He relies on a special formula or secret device to effect his cure.
- He may imply a quick or easy cure.
- He relies heavily on testimonials from his patients.
- He will not allow his methods to be examined by competent medical authorities.
- He scoffs at the practice of medicine and claims that he is being persecuted by medical men.
- He claims that his methods are superior to those used by medical doctors.

The American Medical Association recommends the following precautions to protect your health and your purse from fraud:
- Leave the diagnosis of your ailments to your physician.
- Take medications only under the prescription of your physician.
- Be wary about testimonials. Even genuine cures may not be due to the causes held responsible for them. Spontaneous remission may account for relief which is supposed to have come from another source.
- Watch out for sure cures for ailments like arthritis, for which no known cure has been found.
- Avoid products which promise more than temporary relief for minor arthritis pains.
- Check all medications with your physician before taking them.
- Consult your pharmacist about how to take your medication, and also for other drug information.

HOW TO STRETCH YOUR HEALTH CARE DOLLAR:

1. Have regular checkups; catch complaints before they develop into chronic, life-threatening illnesses.
2. Use the telephone to consult about minor health problems.
3. Know which public health services are available for screening and detection of diseases.
4. Find out about free clinics operated by service-oriented agencies.
5. Avoid confinement in the hospital for diagnostic tests and treatment which could be given as an outpatient.
6. Do not insist on a private room, unless this is important for you, or covered by your insurance.
7. Investigate the possibility of having the services of a visiting nurse before going to the hospital. Room and board are cheaper at home than at the hospital, if all you need is medical attention.
8. Investigate group purchasing plans available to unions, consumer cooperatives, and senior citizens.
9. Ask your doctor to write your prescription in generic terms. This is much cheaper than buying brand names of the same medicine. "A rose by an other name ..." may smell the same, but it costs a lot more if it is part of a name-brand medicine.

"HOW TO SUCCEED ... WITHOUT REALLY TRYING"

Your income in retirement is reduced from what it was before retirement. You would welcome the additional security which the provision of more income, or the protection against greater expense, would afford. Many unscrupulous operators are ready to take advantage of the vulnerable position of the aged by offering much for little.

How can we recognize the schemes which lie in wait to take away our purse? Shakespeare obviously was not writing from the retired person's limited financial resources when he said, "He who steal my purse steal trash ... twas mine, tis his, and has been a slave to millions." Most of us would like to keep our purse intact from the trash who would like to empty it for us!

The following have frequently been traps into which many—including retired individuals—have fallen:

1. **Work-at-home**—These opportunities appear in the newspaper and usually are designed to sell the products which are to be the basis of the lucrative home industry. Sometimes a registration fee is required, following which the applicant is advised that his products do not measure up to the high standards of the promoter.

   The Better Business Bureau warns against the following tactics:
   (a) Help wanted column ads with no offer of employment.
   (b) Offer of huge profits.
   (c) Emphasis on large part-time earnings.
   (d) Use of testimonials with no way to check with the individuals.
   (e) Sell materials, kits, instructions, and equipment at high prices.
   (f) Guaranteed market.
   (g) Exaggerated demand for product.
   (h) Claim that no experience is necessary.

2. **Purchase of franchise**—Newspaper ads used to offer great profits for little work. Exclusive territories, trained personnel to assist, and financial help is promised. Check with bank, lawyer, and Better Business Bureau before investing money.

3. **Chain-referral schemes**—This fraud consists of buying an expensive article with the hope that the purchase of similar articles by friends will result in commissions to reduce the original price.

4. **Vanity publishers**—This fraud involves the publication of a book or recording music which you have written. Victims are led to believe that their works have merit and are encouraged to invest money in the publication or recording.

"I THINK YOU'LL FIND SIR, OUR BROCHURE SAYS SAFE BEACH...**YOU MUST HAVE GONE INTO THE WATER!**"

5. **Land fraud** — Retirement homesites are often the bait for "$1 Down and $10 a Month" ads. The low price is no reason to be less cautious about the purchase. If the land is in an undeveloped area, you should ask yourself these questions:
   (a) Am I prepared to live in an isolated site, far from the city?
   (b) Is medical care available near the site?
   (c) Are utilities and facilities available?
   (d) How close will shopping facilities be?
   (e) Are improvements promised for the land in the near future?
   (f) What taxes will have to be paid?
   (g) What about the title to the land? Is it clear?
   (h) Have I been pressured into making a quick decision?
   (i) Have I seen the land I want to buy? This list goes on and on.
6. **Fake contest** where you have to pay for what you have "won."
7. **Debt consolidation** where the consolidation fee is paid before money is applied to other debts.
8. **Charity rackets:**
   (a) Donate only to known causes and organizations.
   (b) Ask for a financial statement from unfamiliar organizations.
   (c) Check with the Better Business Bureau or Chamber of Commerce.
9. **Fraudulent correspondence schools**— Watch the contract which must be signed, regardless of whether or not the individual wishes to continue with the course.
10. **Memberships** in buyers, discount, recreational, or food distributors clubs, with representations that membership will result in a savings.

By now you're probably ready to bar the door and close the blinds to shield yourself from the hostile world which lurks without! That isn't necessary. Maybe the only protection you need is to be a little bit tougher, yourself.

Be hard to please. Insist on quality and service. Don't believe everything you hear or read. Complain.

That's right. Know how and where to file a complaint when your rights as a consumer have been violated. It is worth the bother.

Many times you can go back to the person who is responsible for the unsatisfactory service or the sale of a faulty product, and a courteous request on your part is all that is necessary.

HOW TO FILE A COMPLAINT

When you report unsatisfactory goods or services, assemble all the information about dates, payments, contracts, receipts, etc., so that there is little room for confusion. You will also impress the individual that you are serious about carrying through with your complaint when he sees that you have gone to all that trouble!

If you cannot get satisfaction from the level where the salesperson operates, find out where the highest authority is to which you can appeal in the store. Keep calm. The fact that you maintain your composure will show that you are confident, and the individuals with whom you talk will know that your complaint will likely be respected if it goes to someone above them.

Letters should be written to the President. State the facts clearly. Keep a copy of everything for your records.

For complaints that cannot be settled using these measures, contact the Bureau of Consumer Fraud and Protection in your State Attorney General's office.

Watch Out for Scams

Telemarketing abuses defraud thousands. It's best not to purchase by phone. Never give your credit card, bank account, or social security number to a telemarketer. Consumers with questions about possible phone-related scams can call the **National Fraud Information Center** at 1-800-876-7060. The center is open Monday to Friday from 9:00 am to 5:30 pm. The line provides recorded information on current frauds and tips on how to avoid becoming a victim. Counselors are also available.

"Consumer's Resource Handbook" is free from the Consumer Information Center, Pueblo, CO 81009. The handbook is a directory of Federal, state and local consumer offices, corporations' consumer offices, trade associations and dispute resolution programs. The revised version will highlight tips on how to use a credit card, complain about a defective product, select a financial institution and choose a school.

"When you've got your health, you've got just about everything," we are told by television commercials. You may not be convinced that this is true, but would you agree that whatever else there is to have is improved by having good health? What about your health? What are your chances of enjoying relatively good health during retirement?

George Gallup reported some time back that 60% of those over 60 were able physically to do almost anything they wanted to do. There is good indication that many people are enjoying full and satisfying lives, usually with some reminder from their body that they are driving a model whose parts don't function like they did when they were brand new.

By age 45, most people have one or more chronic conditions. Of those over 65, 81% report one or more chronic conditions. Only 49% reported any limitation on their activities by the chronic condition. Only 16% reported conditions which inhibited major activity on their part.

PROFILE OF LONGEVITY

The pattern is beginning to come through as data is accumulated from the lives of those who score well in longevity. The man most likely to succeed at living a long time has the following characteristics. Some of the qualities which contribute to long life are not things over which we have control. A few look like they might be ... even now.

- Understanding of one's self: physically, mentally, and socially
- Good medical care in early and later life
- Heredity
- Environment
- Health habits and personal care
- Attitudes
- Coping with stress

Now that you have seen the factors which make people last and last, look at the principal reasons why they don't. To what extent does your good score on the "Longevity Test" above reassure you about your chances of eluding the Four Major Enemies of Man—heart ailments, cancer, stroke, accidents?

"YOU ARE WHAT YOU EAT"

All we mean by the quote is that proper diet will have some effect on your body and your frame of mind. A proper diet is one of the principal contributors to good health. Unfortunately, it is difficult to maintain during the years when your body needs all the help it can get ... during retirement.

Food is expensive, and the reduced budget on which you live may tempt you to "cut corners" at mealtime. Besides, your appetite is not what it once was, and you may have developed a dislike for certain foods. Again, it's just too much bother to prepare food when there are just the two of you (or just yourself).

Food markets are often inaccessible, and their packaged items are often too large for your needs. Your kitchen equipment may not be as adequate as what you once needed, and on and on ... reasons why you don't give your body the nutrients it needs to function well. Examine your diet to see that it provides both the energy and the nutrients you need. Check our suggestions under consumer education for ways of doing this without having to spend extra money on food.

FOOD MAKES THE MAN, OR WOMAN

The average American eats almost 1,500 pounds of food each year. He takes in about 3,000 calories a day, when he could live longer if he reduced his intake by 23% to 2,300. This uniquely American problem of overeating gives the body more fuel than it can burn. It increases fat in the body, which interferes with the movement of muscles and places a burden on the heart. The increased demand for insulin, essential for burning fuel, causes a failure in the cells charged with its production.

TAKE IT OFF

If a major problem is eating too much, it can be corrected by eating less. Not necessarily! A diet is a prescription for a particular physical condition. It should be given the same respect as any other medical recommendation, both in the way it is received and the way it is followed. You don't prescribe medication or go to the inexperienced for medical advice. Don't give or take advice about dieting. "One man's drink is another man's poison" is a disturbing way of reminding us that we are of different compositions and conditions, requiring individual diagnosis and prescription.

About one older adult in three has a chronic health condition that requires diet as part of the treatment. Some of the most common diets have to do with limiting the intake of salt and fat. The large percentage of Americans who are overweight suggests a relationship between the number of diseases which are complicated by excess fat: the tendency toward heart attacks, cerebral hemorrhage, nephritis, and diabetes.

Diet counseling by a dietitian or nutritionist may be helpful in changing poor nutritional habits and adopting diets necessitated by disease. Insufficient exercise, diminished appetites, poor dentation, gastro-intestinal problems, overweight, heart disease and diabetes—each may make specific diet changes necessary. About 50% of Americans have lost all their teeth by age 85.

Good eating habits, including proper diet, will cut heart and vascular diseases by 25%. A decrease in respiratory diseases by 20% and arthritis and diabetes by 50% could be achieved by the proper use of food. Sometimes eating less, but more frequently, enables an individual to achieve the proper quantity of nutrients and energy with a minimum of anguish.

DON'T JUST SIT THERE!!

Exercise is a vital necessity every day. You may be able to store the benefits of eating, but the benefits of exercise cannot be stored for long periods.

The goals of a physical fitness program will be composed of two parts: organic fitness, which includes the condition of the vital organs and limbs of your body; and dynamic fitness, the efficiency of your heart and lungs.

You will be able to tell when your physical fitness program is having its desired effect. (People around you will also be able to tell!) Your attitude toward your work will be more positive and optimistic. Your performance will be improved in what you try to do, and you will accomplish more with less strain and tension.

When your body is functioning properly you will have greater stamina, strength, endurance and coordination. The times when you are "all thumbs" may be those in which you have not maintained a balanced program of exercise. And those joints… how stiff they are after extended periods of inactivty: long trips, long sermons, etc.!! Regular exercise can bring increased flexibility back to most joints. For women, exercise decreases calcium loss from bones thereby helping to prevent osteoporosis.

Chronic fatigue may be due to other causes, but much tiredness can be eliminated by … greater activity! This is not like saying, "Yes, dear, I know you are exhausted from your day on the job, so go right out and hang up this basket of clothes and you'll feel a lot better." Read our suggestions for leisure as they relate to exercise. The right kind of activity (maybe even hanging clothes?!) might be the cure for this fatigue.

An improved and more efficient circulatory system is another effect of a good program. It in itself can be the cause of some of the other good things

we have traced back to sound exercise. Medical authorities suggest that the circulatory system of the average American male white-collar worker aged 25 has already taken on the characteristics which you would expect of a system during middle age.

The latest guidelines from federal health authorities and fitness experts stress that while strenuous exercise (such as jogging or cycling) provides the most benefits, more moderate exercise and even everyday physical activities (gardening, house cleaning, walking to work, or climbing a flight or two of stairs) can also help keep you healthy.

Exercise also reduces the number of calories stored in your body as fat—and therefore keeps weight down and fitness up.

AT EASE!"

Don't overdo your exercises, particularly at the beginning. It took more than a day to get in your present condition, and it may take a while before you begin to look and feel better. Make your routines reasonable and (groan) fun. Join a group. Your local YMCA or high school may have an adult program. Persuade a friend to exercise or work out with you. Get out and exercise with your dog, if you don't want to be seen running alone. Find an exercise show on TV, or do exercises watching the nightly news. Things may sound better with your circulation tuned up! Exercise has been called the conditioner for the healthy and the therapy for the ill.

YOU CAN TURN BACK THE YEARS WITH EXERCISE

So you don't enjoy jogging miles every day—or you can't. You don't get a kick out of exhausting yourself on a tennis court. In fact, you don't do much of anything that involves physical exertion.

You have a problem, but fortunately it is one that can be resolved easily and without cost through regular exercises. As you grow older, they become vital. They are not an illusory Fountain of Youth, but exercises make later years easier and can prolong lives.

A study of 300,000 men over 45 years old found that the death rate among those leading completely sedentary lives was four to five times that of men who exercise regularly. The study confirmed that medically known fact that bodies—both men's and women's—deteriorate without proper exercise. This is so whether you are in your 20's or up in your 70's or 80's. Bodies must be

used. If they aren't, they lose efficiency.

You can delay or reverse many of the deteriorating effects of age by exercising—alone, or even better with your spouse. All it takes is determination. It can be as easy and enjoyable as a half-hour walk four times a week.

WHAT HAPPENS TO YOUR BODY AS YOU GROW OLDER?

Dr. Herbert A. de Vries, director of the exercise laboratory of the Andrus Gerontology Center of the University of Southern California, recently outlined what happens to your body as you age, and how regular exercises can help in coping with changes. According to Dr. de Vries:

- The heart's ability to pump blood declines by about 8% each decade in adulthood, and blood pressure increases as fatty deposits clog arteries. By middle-age, the openings of the coronary arteries are likely to be about 29% smaller than when you were in your mid 20's.
- Lung capacity decreases and the chest wall stiffens as you grow older; this cuts the amount of oxygen available to body tissues and for work and other physical activities. The amount of oxygen you must use at age 75 is ordinarily less than half what it was at 20.
- Skeletal muscles, such as those in arms and legs, gradually lose strength. Tests show that 3% to 5% of muscle tissue is lost every decade. Loss of muscular strength and tissue mean ebbing endurance.
- The proportion of your body that is fat increases. To keep the same proportion of fat to lean body mass (not the way you look outside, but internally) you have to weigh less and less as you grow older.

Don't let these facts about aging and your body worry you too much! Using your body can mitigate and delay the wearing processes. You can continue to be young in spite of your calendar years.

Exercise can enhance the body's vigor and increase its work capacity. It can help the heart deliver more blood and oxygen for body tissues, slow the conversion of lean body mass to fat, and even strengthen bones. It tends to stave off the aging of nerve cells, and according to some medical opinion, it can slow down or avert arthritic changes in hips, knees, and other joints.

Swimming (a minimum quarter-mile), bicycling, folk and other dancing on a regular basis, and some less vigorous sports are good for everyone. So is gardening and—homemakers insist—work in the home.

Don't forget an exercise you do—or should do every day: walking. Walking has been long overlooked as an excellent exercise for the heart, muscles, and lungs, and can have added benefits as well. Walking can give you a chance to relax, enjoy your surroundings, and give you a much-needed "breath of fresh air." You should build up your walking distance slowly, keeping your pace fast without becoming out of breath. Try increasing the distance you walk until you think you have exercised enough—45 minutes is a good top amount for some.

GET MOVING — BUT DO IT WISELY

We all would like to feel better and have our bodies at their best. What comes easiest for most of us is a regimen of regular exercise in the home: to tone muscles, help prevent a sagging posture, stimulate digestion and bodily processes, maintain blood circulation and respiration, and help keep the heart strong and the joints flexible.

Such a routine can be highly effective and, once you get into the swing of it, enjoyable and relaxing.

A word of caution: whatever you do, especially if you are over 40, should be undertaken with medical advice. This can be critical if an exercise program or involvement in a sport is strenuous, and it is important even for an exercise program in the home. Your doctor may want to suggest special exercises for you, or he may want to caution you against undertaking too much.

WHEN YOU'RE SET FOR YOUR HOME ROUTINE ...

Exercise or physical fitness programs can be worked out for anyone—the middle-aged, the healthy aging and those with special health needs. Sit-down exercises for those who spend their days in wheelchairs or are otherwise sedentary are particularly important, as are exercises for the bedridden.

The Maryland Commission on Physical Fitness, with the help of the National Association for Human Development and the Maryland Office on Aging, has developed "The Basic Ten," a fitness program featured in an activity guide by the Michigan Office of Services to the Aging.

Before beginning the "Basic Ten":
- See your doctor first.
- Warm up before exercising. Breathe deeply, rising up on your toes slowly with arms extended over your head, then exhale slowly. Three times should do it. Also walk in place, lifting knees high in turn for ten times.
- Do your exercises slowly, and do not do too much for too long at first. Stop if you begin hurting anywhere or get tired. Increase your regimen gradually.
- Take deep breaths between exercises.
- You may feel some dizziness, which you can avoid by resting before alternating sides in an exercise.
- 15 to 20 minutes a day will give you a good workout. Dr. de Vries suggests that you lie flat after each workout and take 15 minutes of yoga-like exercises: stretching leg muscles by bending legs from the hip and knee, tensing them as much as you can and holding them down with your arms.

Now, take a look at the "Basic Ten." Good luck, and happy exercising!

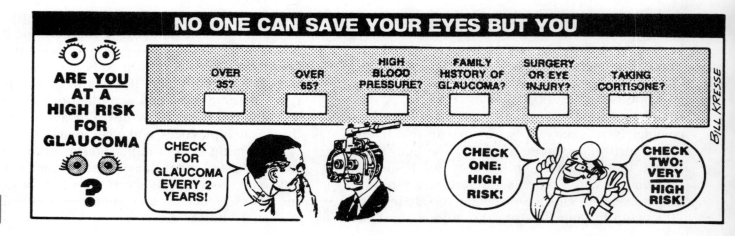

1 **Arm Swings**—Swing right arm rotating forward 5 times; reverse motion, rotating backward 5 times. Repeat with left arm. With both arms together in a windmill fashion swing forward 5 times.

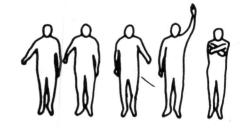

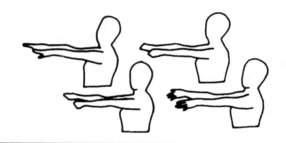

2 **Finger Squeeze**—Extend arms shoulder height in front, palms down; squeeze the fingers slowly, then release. Repeat 5 times. Then turn palms up, squeeze fingers 5 times. Extend arms again in front and shake fingers 5 times.

3 **Arm Turns**—Extend arms to the side, palms up, cup hands, turn arms down in a circular movement and return to starting position. Repeat 5 times. Extend arms, cup hands, facing down, turn arms in the opposite direction 5 times.

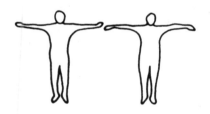

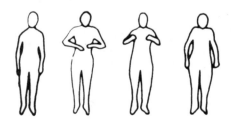

4 **Shoulder Rolls**—Beginning with arms at side, roll shoulders forward in full circle, slowly, 5 times; reverse by rolling shoulders backwards in a circle, slowly, 5 times. Then shrug shoulders up and down 5 times.

5 **Body Stretch**—Extend right foot forward as far as it will go, leaving the left foot firmly planted; bend body forward with arms extended, stretch forward 5 counts, stretching further forward on each count. Reverse procedure. Lift up on your toes, stretch your arms overhead to a count of 5.

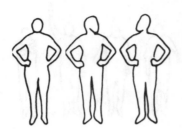

Head & Neck Exercise—Place hands on hips. Bend forward so that chin touches the chest. Then bend head to starting position and slowly turn the head to the left, return head to starting position and then slowly turn head to the right. Repeat 5 times.

6

Easy Back Stretch—Sit part way off the seat of a straight chair. Relax your body and let your head drop between your knees. Your shoulders should rest on your knees, your hands will hang alongside your legs. BREATHE NATURALLY while you relax in this position for two or three minutes, or less if the position becomes difficult. Then bring your hands up to your knees again, and **using your arms for support,** begin to curl yourself up to a sitting position, with your head straightening last.

7

Body Side Stretch—Place left hand on left hip, extend right arm over head, bend to left side toward the ground, to the count of two. Return to starting position and place right hand on right hip with left arm extended upward over head and bend to the right, to count of 2.

8

9

Posture Exercise—Stand erect with feet about six inches apart. Tighten leg muscles, tighten stomach by drawing it in, extend chest, bring arms up with clenched fists chest high, take deep breath, let it out slowly (keeping the muscles taut and rigid) vibrate arms back for a count of 3.

Arm Stretch—With feet six inches apart, make fists, bend elbows, then thrust arms forward, bring back; thrust sideways, bring back, then thrust arms upward and down. Repeat 3 times.

10

Drawings by Mary Effie Burnham

"AN APPLE A DAY, PLUS ..."

Preventative health measures include more than the regular consumption of apples. There are precautions we can take to reduce the probability that we will lose our health through sickness or accidents. We can increase our resistance to illness and make early detection and treatment work against many disabilities.

"EARLY TO BED ..."

It isn't so important what time you get there, as it is how long you stay there. Older people generally need less rest than middle-aged and younger people. Individual requirements differ, but 7-8 hours during a 24-hour period is about average. Scientists have observed that cumulative sleep loss adds up to nervousness and sometimes to psychosomatic illness. Chronic inability to sleep suggests the need for a doctor's attention. Too much sleep can be a problem, indicating boredom or an illness.

SOME TIPS FOR GETTING A GOOD NIGHT'S SLEEP

We must stress that if you are bothered by something more than occasional trouble falling asleep and sleeping well, if it is a frequently recurring, long-lasting chronic problem that you can't shake, then you should see your doctor. It is better to be assured that you haven't anything to worry about than to find out later that you have a problem that requires professional treatment.

HAZARDS

Drs. Joyce and Anthony Kales, who conduct sleep research at the Hershey Medical Center of Pennsylvania State University, have found that many chronic insomniacs keep their problems to themselves—"bottled up inside"—without venting anger, frustrations and disappointments.

Tension, stress and anxiety build-up are carried into the night. They are likely to cause racing thoughts, activate the physical arousal system and make it difficult to get to sleep, according to the Kales; body temperature and heart rates go up for disturbed chronic insomniacs, and can lead to neurotic depression and other emotional problems. In some cases, chronic insomnia can be traced to illnesses such as angina or asthma or other respiratory disorders, or to back problems or arthritis. Those who suffer from persistent sleeplessness should see their doctor. Prescribed medication often helps. For those seriously affected, there are clinics around the country where technicians can diagnose sleep problems and help resolve them. Otherwise, here are some suggestions distilled from programs that have been outlined by Dr. Donald Douglas of the Lenox Hill Hospital in New York, Drs. Joyce and Anthony Kales of the Pennsylvania Hershey Medical Center, Wallace Mendelson of the National Institute of Mental Health and others in the field:

- Recognize that sleep needs differ; you may be among those who need less than a seven and one-half hour norm.
- Go to bed and get up about the same time every day, weekends included.
- If you go to bed and don't feel sleepy, try to lull yourself to sleep with a book that isn't so absorbing that it keeps you awake instead of making you sleepy. Or turn on a radio to quiet, soothing music.
- Drink hot milk. It has an essential amino acid that has been used medically to treat depression and as a sedative. Although milk has only a small amount of amino acid (medically referred to as L-tryptophan) it often helps assure restful

ZZZZZZZZZZZ • DO'S AND DONT'S ABOUT SLEEP!

sleep. Medical tests have also supported the sedative value of a mild "hot toddy" of whiskey, water and perhaps lemon juice, or wine or brandy. Go easy, though, stronger drinks act as a stimulant.

- Relax in bed; try to lie absolutely still. Dr. Douglas says the body resists not moving a muscle but moving, trying to find a sleep-provoking position, usually means having to start again on relaxing the body and the mind.

- Concentrate on breathing, inhaling and exhaling deeper and at regular intervals, think of your breathing, trying to keep your mind clear of disturbing thoughts; your grandmothers probably called this "counting sheep."

- As much as anything, don't try to force sleep. The more you struggle to go to sleep or worry about wakefulness, the harder it will be to get to sleep. It can be better to surrender and stay awake a while longer.

- Don't resort to pills unless they've been prescribed by your doctor. While over-the-counter remedies to promote quick sleep and restful nights can be useful for occasional sleeplessness, the National Institute of Health has warned that sleeping pills or even mild remedies can be harmful if overused. If you can tolerate aspirin, you might try it as a relaxant at bedtime when you need one.

For more information on sleep difficulties, write to the National Sleep Foundation at 1367 Connecticut Avenue, NW, Suite 200, Box RON, Washington, DC 20036 and ask for copies of its free brochures on sleep disorders.

S TOP SMOKING

Smokers are becoming a minority—only one-third of adults are now cigarette smokers. If you still smoke, now's the time to join the more than 30 million ex-smokers, and the majority. Smoking is an expensive habit, both in terms of your health and your wealth. It's responsible for more cancer-related deaths than any other single agent, and it's a contributing factor in emphysema, bronchitis, and heart attack.

You know you should quit. But let's accentuate the positive. Think of the benefits of quitting now.

When you quit smoking, your body starts to repair itself almost immediately. You enter lower risk groups. You lose your smoker's hacking cough, and related head and stomach aches. You recover

your sense of taste and smell. And at over $1 a pack, smoking is one habit you can afford to lose.

The American Cancer Society has information to help you. Contact your local chapter.

M ENTAL HEALTH

The relationship that exists between mental and physical conditions is too complicated to discuss at length in this chapter. Most of us have sensed the effect which illness in one area has upon well-being in the other. The person with a healthy self-concept and social adjustment will not be completely protected from poor health. There are certain characteristics, however, which tend to accompany those who cope successfully with life's problems, not only during aging, but throughout all of life. Just as you have probably faced crises or problematic situations during your life, you will face them in retirement and cope with them as effectively as you did earlier.

P ROFILE OF A HEALTHY LIFE

There is evidence that people with the following traits tend to adjust and cope better than those who lack them. Check those that could be descriptions of you:

_____ Has an enduring and honest affection for others
_____ Is independent
_____ Finds satisfying outlets for time and energy
_____ Enjoys life
_____ Has a sense of usefulness
_____ Avoids self-pity

I NVISIBLE SUPPORTS

The person who discovers meaning in life has resources which are not known to the skeptic. Some individuals develop these through their life experiences, while others are sustained by confidence in God. Dr. Carl Jung, one of psychiatry's founders, said, "Among all my patients, in the second half of life … that is to say, over thirty-five, there has not been one whose problem in the last resort was not that of finding a religious outlook on life. It is safe to say that every one of them feel ill because he had lost that which the living religions of every age have given their followers, and none of them has really been healed who did not regain his religious outlook."

LIVING WITH STRESS: STUDIES ARE UNRAVELING THE MYSTERIES OF STRESS

Few of us escape stress in our daily lives. It's commonplace. Most of us take it for granted—but we shouldn't.

Stress is the body's physical and chemical reaction to anything that frightens, excites, confuses or endangers a person. No matter what you do on the job or away from it, you frequently come under mental or physical stress. It seems unavoidable in these days of high-pressure, fast-paced lives, with rapid changes, uncertainties and anxieties about jobs, rising living costs and growing family responsibilities.

While stress is not necessarily a medical problem, it can be. It must be watched.

Stress that can be endured promotes physical and mental development and growth. The adrenaline pumped into the blood stream at such times can give the extra strength needed to achieve more—to endure more, work harder and more creatively.

Stress can be a prod but if it gets out of hand it can be harmful.

Studies conducted by the Harvard University Medical School, Boston University and Northwestern University are finding strong evidence that prolonged and excessive stress can be serious—even a killer. It can make men and women more susceptible to a wide variety of diseases, including cancer.

In its milder forms, stress usually leads to nothing worse than a persistent case of the "blahs," or general unhappiness and depression and nagging anxieties. The serious problems come when stress is allowed to become distress—when the body and mind no longer can handle it. Once it passes the level of tolerance, it becomes a potential medical problem. It can cause changes in the body's immune system, the body's built-in defense against illness, and reduce the body's ability to fight virus-infected cells. According to Harvard's Dr. Steve Locke, this can "pre-dispose a person to illness."

THE OLDER YOU ARE, THE MORE VULNERABLE YOU ARE

Stress affects the old and the young but because the young usually have more physical resilience and reserves, they are better able to cope with it. Studies show that those approaching retirement, men and women, or retirees are the most vulnerable.

As we grow older, says Dr. Ruth B. Weg of the University of California's Andrus Gerontology Center, we have "a diminishing ability to respond to stress." It hits harder and recovery from it takes longer.

We must watch ourselves more closely as we grow older, learn to recognize the symptoms of stress and learn to cope with it before it builds up dangerously.

HOW TO RECOGNIZE THE SYMPTOMS OF SERIOUS STRESS

Unfortunately, too many of us do not recognize the signs of stress or pay too little attention to them. For far too many, it's a natural part of the wear and tear of life—something that must be endured.

Recognizing the signs of stress is the first step toward coping with it effectively.

What are the symptoms? "Butterflies" in the stomach. Tension and nervousness over prolonged periods. Light perspiration when things don't seem to be going right. Headaches. A feeling of pressure on the back of the neck. Heavy breathing. Or an "internal racing" and pounding heart.

We may be alerted to stress by insomnia, ulcers and other stomach troubles. We may find it's the cause of hypertension and heart strain, or a change to an unhealthy pattern of behavior, such as excessive smoking, drinking or eating in search of relief. A sudden urge for snacking could mean stress!

Once you recognize that stress is a problem that must be dealt with, you can minimize the way it affects you.

HOW YOU CAN EASE THE PRESSURES OF STRESS

Start by seeking the cause of stress.

Often it's obvious. Sometimes it isn't.

The death or serious illness of a spouse is considered by psychologists to be the most serious cause of stress. On a scale of 100, other causes are rated substantially lower.

The loss of a spouse, or the death of a close relative or friend, is the hardest to handle. Help should be sought.

Other major causes of stress include retirement—rated high on the stress scale because of the upheaval it causes in personal lives—and illness and accidents, marital troubles and divorce, sexual

TEST YOUR STRESS LEVEL

Score Yourself: Never = 0;
Seldom = 1; Frequently = 2

How often do you feel:

Strong anxiety ....( )
Irritable over little things............................( )
Frustrated ....( )
Quick anger..( )
A desire to avoid people...............................( )
A difficulty in concentrating ....( )
Easily disturbed or startled..........................( )
Jittery, unable to sit still ....( )
Unusually emotional ....( )
Depressed ....( )
A loss of interest in everything ....( )
Persistently keyed up ....( )

How often do you experience:

General fatigue..( )
Sleeplessness at night...................................( )
Heart pounding..( )
Headaches ....( )
Breathing difficulties....................................( )
Burping, gassiness, acid stomach.................( )
Frequent need to urinate...............................( )
Tense head and neck muscles ....( )
Grinding of teeth ....( )
Dry mouth or throat ....( )
Sudden perspiration ....( )
Cold hands or feet if it's warm,
    sweaty hands or feet otherwise ....( )

Add the point totals in the two columns: If together they are 10 or under, you are normal; if 10 to 20, take care; if higher, you could have a problem.

changes, work-related problems and changes in living conditions.

Unlike the death of a spouse, these are seldom serious enough, alone, to cause major problems. The trouble is, when one stressful situation comes, others often follow it. The loss of a job, 47 on the stress scale, can cause financial problems, disrupt living patterns and lead to all sorts of satellite problems, sending the stress count above 200—recognized as a critical level.

Studies that have concentrated on the causes of serious stress have found, typically, that 27% of one large group interviewed intensively had experienced "high levels of psychic distress" over a year's time as a result of snowballing causes of stress, a steady buildup.

Acting quickly helps to avoid that.

Stress takes two basic forms: Mental stress and physical stress.

● Mental stress is a "bad" stress, caused primarily by emotional disturbances, frustrations or anxieties—things over which we have little or no control. They build on each other, can be serious and need prompt attention.

● Physical stress is a "good" stress, as long as you don't overexert yourself. While it can be serious in later years, it can also be relaxing and an antidote for mental stress.

Rest is good in cases of physical stress—but physical activity, even to a point of careful stress, is helpful when mental stress is a problem. Don't

sit and worry; do something that involves physical activity.

In retirement, recognize that boredom from inactivity is stressful; work it off. Such everyday activities as gardening, chores around the home, walking or a physical hobby will suffice.

Exertion is not always necessary. The concentration needed for chess or some other game, a crossword puzzle or reading can help.

Often, simply blowing off steam can help relieve stress. Repressed anger, frustration and anxiety make it build up in daily life. Some therapists advocate going into a room, closing doors and windows, and letting off a "primal scream" to ease pressures. That sounds extreme. Find your own way, but get rid of stress—and work out ways to avoid its return.

Stress, particularly that leading to muscular contractions and aches and tension headaches, can be eased by medication, usually aspirin if you can take it, but don't be a pill-popper. Medication may ease stress symptoms but it does not attack the cause of the stress, and it can be habit-forming and thus lead to a different form of personal stress.

Consider aspirin or anti-depressant or anti-anxiety drugs (they should be prescribed by a doctor) as only temporary relief for stress. Seek real relief not from pills but from adjustments to the causes of the stress you feel.

Rest is important to relieve physical stress. It can also be important in situations involving men-

Rest is important to relieve physical stress. It can also be important in situations involving mental and emotional stress: Lack of sleep or relaxing rest aggravates tensions and the body's ability to throw them off. However, sleep does not necessarily attack the causes of stress; the tension headaches or tight muscles you have at bedtime often return after you wake.

Stress also leads to night wakefulness. If you can't get the seven or eight hours of sleep you need, consult your doctor.

If you can isolate what is bothering you, the cause of your stress, try to work out a solution. If there are a number of causes, work on them one at a time, the most important first. Make up your mind to accept what you cannot change, problems beyond your control, until you are better able to do something about them.

Too often, a person who feels beset by problems becomes so involved with them, so mentally and emotionally tense, that he or she fails to see ways out of the situation.

If you can't seem to work things out, talk to a sympathetic listener, someone you respect and trust. It will help put things in better perspective. The listener can be a member of your family, a friend, a clergyman or teacher, someone in the personnel office, or your doctor. If professional counseling seems wise, there are Family Service and other similar agencies available, with social workers trained to help.

Don't feel ashamed, embarrassed or guilty about going to a professional for assistance; it's not an admission of personal inadequacy but a mark of intelligence to seek advice wherever it can be found.

Dr. Steve Locke of Harvard says, "to the extent that an individual has effective coping strategies and social psychological resources to rely on, stress should cause less deterioration of health and well-being."

WHAT YOU CAN DO WHEN YOU FEEL STRESS BUILDING UP

You know when stress is building up inside. As soon as you do, you should do something about it.

Try to relax. Slow down: Don't rush your life away. As a cardiologist put it, don't let yourself become a heart-attack-prone person—one who is hurried, aggressive, impatient and easily angered. A more relaxed person lives a far more pleasant and healthier life.

A more formal way of relaxing is the "rag doll" technique. Sit on the edge of a straight chair, knees about 12 inches apart, legs slanted out 10 or 12 inches in front of the chair. Sit straight and then collapse forward, back rounded, hands resting on your knees. Let your mind concentrate on parts of your body, relaxing each in turn, breathing deeply. Do it whenever you feel a need to ease body tensions. It will work.

This can mean ridding yourself of trivial obligations to concentrate on what is most important to you.

Cultivate diversions, such as concerts, plays, visits to museums, visits with friends—and sports as a spectator rather than as a fiercely competitive participant.

Learn to enjoy your own company; do nothing rather than rush to keep up with a full calendar.

Learn a few secrets that can help fight stress. One is a quick-quieting, ten second breathing exer-

WHAT YOU CAN DO WHEN YOU FEEL STRESS COMING ON!

TALK IT OUT! — LET'S DO THIS! / GOOD IDEA! / HONK!

RELAX! — SCREECH! / HONK! / BEEP!

PLAN! — ...AND ROSES! / TULIPS! / SPRING PLANTING

ENJOY! — THIS IS A DELICIOUS RECIPE! / THANK YOU!

BILL KRESSE

cise: When you feel stress coming on, take two slow, easy, deep breaths and exhale slowly, a count of four in, four out, four in and four out again. As you exhale, let your body go limp. Let your mind relax, also. You can feel better immediately once you learn to relax completely.

In prolonged periods of stress, this can be done frequently during the day—but it shouldn't be allowed to become a scheduled exercise, every half-hour or hour, say, but one to be enjoyed as a "break" in times of pressure.

COPING WITH DEPRESSION
GOT THE BLUES?
DOWN IN THE DUMPS?
WATCH OUT!

"You've got a bad case of the blues."

"I'm down deep in the dumps."

You hear people say such things. Chances are you say them yourself at times. It happens to everyone.

If it doesn't hang on, if it is a mood that comes and goes, you can fight it off by thinking and acting positively. If it doesn't go away, you should be aware that depression can be a major mental health problem.

It affects more than your mood. It can manifest itself in symptoms as diverse as sleeplessness (you lie awake worrying about real or fancied problems), boredom, inertia and an inability to concentrate, impatience and irritability and not uncommonly stress.

It can affect your appetite; you might lose interest in food.

It can lead to more smoking or drinking. It can be a factor in driving; accident records indicate that drivers suffering from depression are more likely to be reckless and to lack the concentration vital for safety. And, similarly, it can affect performance on the job.

All in all, while you can shrug off an occasional case of the blues, if depression takes over you should recognize it as a health problem to be dealt with professionally.

Don't let it control you.

BLUES OR DEPRESSION?
CHECK YOUR SYMPTOMS

New York University's Medical Center has been conducting intensive research into depression during the past few decades through its Millhauser Laboratories. According to Irene Chang, coordinator of the depression studies program, which works particularly with depressed persons over 55, this research has resulted in "more accurate diagnoses and more effective treatments."

Chang has circulated a check-list of possible symptoms that warrant the attention of those 55 or older—and younger persons who might benefit from early recognition of depression problems.

The symptoms of depression include:

- A low mood—feeling sad, blue and/or hopeless much of the time.
- Appetite disturbance—a poor appetite or an increased appetite.
- Sleep problems—difficulties falling asleep, waking up during the night or waking early.
- Lack of energy—quickly fatigued, tired for no reason, tense with difficulty relaxing.
- Loss of interest in usual activities.
- Feelings of self-reproach or inappropriate guilt.

BEAT DEPRESSION

DON'T KNOCK YOURSELF!

SHARE YOUR FEELINGS WITH OTHERS!

GIVE YOURSELF CREDIT FOR WHAT YOU'VE ACCOMPLISHED!

DIPLOMA

● Trouble concentrating and possible difficulties making decisions.

● Excessive thoughts of death or that life is not worth living.

The Millhauser Laboratories study has led to a warning that if you have checked off four or more of the eight items above, you may be suffering from depression. You should check further with your physician or your nearby medical center.

MORE LIKELY, YOU JUST HAVE THE BLUES: GET RID OF THEM

The symptoms for the plain old blues or blahs, or whatever, are much the same as those for more serious forms of depression. The big difference is how persistent the occurrences are and in how many ways the symptoms show up.

Millions of Americans suffer now and then from the blues. Worrying minds make them sleepless, sap their strength, cause them to lose interest in food and usual interests and otherwise have an impact like that of symptoms of depression. However, in most instances you can fight off the blues.

It's not always easy. You have to concentrate on positive thinking instead of worrying through the night about troubles you can do nothing about as, awake, you toss and turn.

NYU's Depression Studies Program suggests:

● Don't knock yourself.

● Don't build up a problem by going over it time and again; you're likely to make it worse, not better.

● Share your feelings with others; your spouse, a relative, a friend or a consultant is likely to have good advice.

● Don't use your age as an excuse for being "down" mentally or physically.

● Give yourself credit for what you've accomplished through the years—and what you can continue to contribute.

● If your blues are about imminent retirement, get rid of them; approach retirement positively as something you can make comfortable and happy.

ELDERCARE LOCATOR

The Eldercare Locator is a nationwide service for older people and caregivers. If you need information on the local availability of legal assistance, housing, adult day care, home health care, or any other type of service, you can call the Locator's toll-free number, 1-800-677-1116, and be put in touch with someone in your area who can help. The program is a collaborative project of the U.S. Administration on Aging, the National Association of Area Agencies on Aging, and the National Association of State Units on Aging.

MEDICARE

Medicare is a health insurance program under Social Security which helps millions of Americans, 65 and older, and many severely disabled people under 65, to pay the high cost of medical care. It has two parts—hospital insurance and medical insurance.

The hospital insurance part of Medicare helps pay for inpatient hospital care and for certain follow-up care after you leave the hospital. The medical insurance part of Medicare helps pay for your doctor's services, outpatient hospital services and many other medical items and services not covered under hospital insurance. (See page 55.)

You don't have to retire to get hospital insurance. If you are eligible for Social Security benefits, you are also eligible for hospital insurance free at age 65, **but you must enroll.** Check with your Social Security office about three months before you reach age 65.

People 65 or older who have not worked long enough to be entitled to hospital insurance can buy this protection by paying a monthly premium for this coverage and for medical insurance.

Anyone who is 65 or older can get medical insurance (Part B of Medicare). If you want it, you pay a monthly premium for it. Medical insurance has a 7-month initial enrollment period. This period begins 3 months before the month you become eligible for medical insurance and ends 3 months after that month. If you turn down medical insurance and then decide you want it after your 7-month initial enrollment period ends, you can sign up during a general enrollment period—January 1 through March 31 of each year. If you enroll during a general enrollment period, however, your medical insurance protection won't start until the following July, and your premium will be 10 percent higher for each 12-month period you could have been enrolled but were not.

Anyone receiving monthly Social Security or Railroad Retirement benefits is automatically enrolled in Part B of Medicare (Medical Insurance) upon attainment of age 65. There is a monthly premium.

MEDICAID

Medicaid is a program of assistance to those in need of medical services which they cannot afford. There is no age requirement for Medicaid. Medicare coverage begins at age 65 but does not cover nursing home custodial care which can be costly.

There are income and net-worth limits for Medicaid eligibility. States differ in their requirements. Essentially a Medicaid recipient and spouse may have a certain income and keep a certain amount of assets including one's home to rec[...] Medicaid. Medicaid rules are very complica[...] Check with your attorney, senior center, or y[...] local government Office of Aging for spec[...] details. Check now so you're prepared when ar[...] you may need Medicaid in the future. **It is imp[...] tant to know that you are not expected[...] exhaust your life savings, go into debt, or [...] your home before receiving Medicaid.**

MEDIGAP INSURANCE POLICIES; SUPPLEMENTAL MEDICARE COVERAGE

As a result of government action, the National Association of Insurance Commissioners drew up ten easy-to-understand Medigap policies. The new policies have a graduated amount of coverage and range in cost from $400 to $1,800 per year.

All policies cover a basic core of benefits that pay the patient's share of Medicare's approved amount for physician services after the $100 annual deductible, the patient's cost of a long hospital stay ($174 a day for 60-90 days, $348 per day for 91-150 days, all approved costs not paid by Medicare after day 150 to a total of 365 days life-time) and charges for the first three pints of bl[...] not covered by Medicare. The cost for this b[...] plan ranges from approximately $400 to $80[...] year. Shop around. More expensive plans, [...] include coverage for items you may never ne[...] may not be the best plans for you. If you are e[...] ble for Medicaid you need not have a Medi[...] policy.

IMPORTANT: You cannot be turned d[...] for Medigap insurance if you apply within [...] months after you reach age 65. After th[...] insurers are free to turn you down.

THE NEW MEDIGAP POLICIES Estimated policies costs. Don't buy more than one policy!!	$400 to $800	$500 to $900	$500 to $900	$550 to $1000	$700 to $1000	$700 to $900	$500 to $700	$700 to $900	$1000 to $1400	$1200 to $1800
	A	**B**	**C**	**D**	**E**	**F**	**G**	**H**	**I**	**J**
Basic	✓	✓	✓	✓	✓	✓	✓	✓	✓	✓
Skilled nursing co-insurance			✓	✓	✓	✓	✓	✓	✓	✓
Part A (hospital) deductible		✓	✓	✓	✓	✓	✓	✓	✓	✓
Part B (doctors' bills) deductible				✓		✓				✓
Doctors' charges beyond Medicare limits						100%	80%		100%	100%
Foreign travel			✓	✓	✓	✓	✓	✓	✓	✓
At-home recovery				✓			✓		✓	✓
Prescription drugs								✓[1]	✓[1]	✓[2]
Preventive care					✓					✓

Shop around for the right policy for you

Your first choice is whether you want a plan that would cover Medicare's hospital deductible. Plan A doesn't cover it; Plan B does.

If you expect to do any foreign travel, consider Plans C-J, which include emergency coverage while abroad. Plans C-J also include skilled nursing co-insurance. Other choices: whether you want the $100 Part B deductible covered (plan C) or benefits for at-home recovery care (D) or preventative care (E).

If one of your doctors bills beyond Medicare limits, look at Plans F and G. F pays $100 or the difference, while G pays 80%; each plan covers slightly different benefits.

Plans H and I cover a variety of benefits including a moderate drug benefit.

Plan J covers all benefits offered plus a higher end drug benefit.

1. $1,250 maximum benefits
2. $3,000 maximum benefits
Note: Policy costs are estimates.

MEDICARE (PART A) HOSPITAL INSURANCE
COVERED SERVICES PER BENEFIT PERIOD[1]

Service	Benefits	Medicare Pays**	You Pay**
HOSPITALIZATION Semi-private room and board, general nursing, and miscellaneous hospital services and supplies	First 60 days 61st day to 90th day 91st day to 150th day* Beyond 150 days	All but $716 All but $179 per day All but $358 per day Nothing	$716 $179 per day $358 per day All costs
POST HOSPITAL SKILLED NURSING FACILITY CARE In a facility approved by Medicare. You must have been in a hospital for at least 3 days and enter the facility within 30 days after hospital discharge (2) and with the same diagnosis as leaving the hospital	First 20 days	100% of approved amount	Nothing
	Additional 80 days	All but $89.50 per day	$89.50 per day
	Beyond 100 days	Nothing	All costs
HOME HEALTH CARE Medicare pays intermittent visits for skilled nursing care or physical therapy	Unlimited visits as medically necessary	Full Cost	Nothing
HOSPICE CARE	Two 90-day periods and one 30-day period	All but limited costs for outpatient drugs and inpatient respite care	Limited cost sharing for outpatient drugs and inpatient respite care
BLOOD	Blood	All but first 3 pints	For first 3 pints

People not eligible for Social Security benefits can purchase Medicare Part A Hospital Insurance for $261 per month (for those with less than 30 credits) or $183 per month (for those with 30-39 credits).

* 60 Reserve Days may be used only once: days used are not renewable.

** These figures are subject to change each year.

(1) A benefit Period begins on the first day you receive service as an inpatient in a hospital and ends after you have been out of the hospital or skilled nursing facility for 60 days in a row.

(2) Medicare and private insurance will not pay for most nursing home care. You pay for custodial care and most care in a nursing home. There are now some policies on the market which will pay for all nursing home costs but they are very expensive.

(3) Medicare pays processing costs; if you have donors to replace the blood, it would cost you nothing.

MEDICARE (PART B) MEDICAL INSURANCE *
COVERED SERVICES PER BENEFIT YEAR

Service	Benefits	Medicare Pays	You Pay
MEDICAL EXPENSE Physician's services, inpatient and outpatient medical services and supplies, physical and speech therapy, ambulance, chiropractic (limited), occupational therapy, durable medical equipment, prosthetic devices, second opinion before surgery, podiatrist's services, diagnostic laboratory tests, etc.	Medicare pays for medical services in or out of the hospital. Some insurance policies pay less (or nothing) for hospital outpatient medical services or services in a doctor's office	80% of approved amount (after $100 deductible)	$100 deductible ** plus 20% of balance of approved amount (Plus any charge above approved amount) ***
HOME HEALTH CARE Intermittent visits for skilled nursing care of physical therapy	Unlimited visits as medically necessary	Full Cost	Nothing
OUTPATIENT HOSPITAL TREATMENT	Unlimited as medically necessary	80% of approved amount (after $100 deductible)	Subject to deductible plus 20% of balance of approved amount
BLOOD	Blood	80% of approved amount (after first 3 pints)	For first 3 pints ††† plus 20% of balance of approved amount

* Available at a monthly premium: in 1995, $46.10; in 1996, $50.20; in 1997, $56.00; in 1998, $62.20.

** Once you have paid $100 for covered services, the Part B deductible does not apply to further covered services you receive the rest of the year.

*** You pay for charges greater than the amount approved by Medicare, unless the doctor or supplier agrees to accept Medicare's approved amount as the total charge for services rendered. Always ask you doctor or supplier to accept assignment. Assignment means the doctor or supplier accepts as full payment whatever the Medicare allowed charge is, and can bill you only the $100 deductible, if not already paid, plus the 20% co-insurance.

††† There is only one deductible for blood each year. If you meet the blood deductible under Part A, you do not have to meet it again under Part B.

CHECKLIST FOR HEALTH

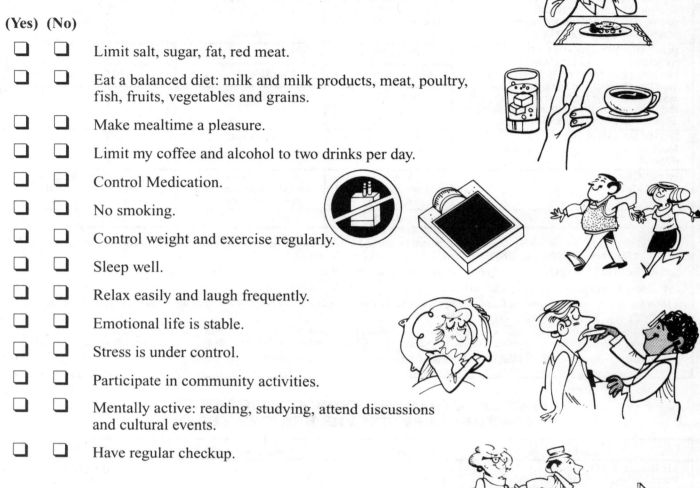

(Yes) (No)

❑ ❑ Limit salt, sugar, fat, red meat.

❑ ❑ Eat a balanced diet: milk and milk products, meat, poultry, fish, fruits, vegetables and grains.

❑ ❑ Make mealtime a pleasure.

❑ ❑ Limit my coffee and alcohol to two drinks per day.

❑ ❑ Control Medication.

❑ ❑ No smoking.

❑ ❑ Control weight and exercise regularly.

❑ ❑ Sleep well.

❑ ❑ Relax easily and laugh frequently.

❑ ❑ Emotional life is stable.

❑ ❑ Stress is under control.

❑ ❑ Participate in community activities.

❑ ❑ Mentally active: reading, studying, attend discussions and cultural events.

❑ ❑ Have regular checkup.

BE PREPARED WITH...

...A FIRST AID COURSE,...

...A CPR COURSE ...

...AND KEEP EMERGENCY NUMBERS HANDY!

DOCTOR 762-7931
HOSPITAL 123-4567

WHERE WILL YOU LIVE?
THE BIG QUESTION:
TO MOVE OR NOT TO MOVE?

Where will we live when we're retired?

Should we move or stay here?

If we move, where should we go?

Those are probably the most discussed questions when husbands and wives begin looking ahead to settling down into retirement life. They are very serious questions: The right decision could determine how comfortable, happy and secure retirement will be.

Americans are the most mobile men and women in the civilized world. Moving is a way of life because of job changes and transfers. Studies have shown that the average American changes homes every four years, most often within the same community but frequently into homes in other cities and states.

This mobility means that families and friends more often than not are scattered around the country—typically brothers and sisters in Virginia, a daughter in New England, another daughter in Washington State and a son still at home with soon-to-retire parents in New Jersey.

The wide separation of families and friends is a sharp American contrast to well-rooted, close-knit families and communities abroad. A natural consequence, as retirement approaches, is to consider moving closer to children, grandchildren, other relatives, or good friends who have moved away.

But should you?

There are many factors to be considered in addition to a natural desire to be closer to where family and friends are located. It's not enough to say, "It'd be good to be nearer the kids."

Remember this: Their way of life may not be yours; their friends might not become your friends, if they should decide to seek better job opportunities elsewhere, you might be left behind and lonelier than ever.

Start thinking early about where you would be happiest in retirement, never losing this important focus: Where you live in retirement will be a critical factor in what you do for the extra income you might need, for personal relationships, for leisure activities, for health and comfort, and so on and on. Explore your options, studying all the options.

It is not too early to think about all of this if retirement is still 10 years in the future.

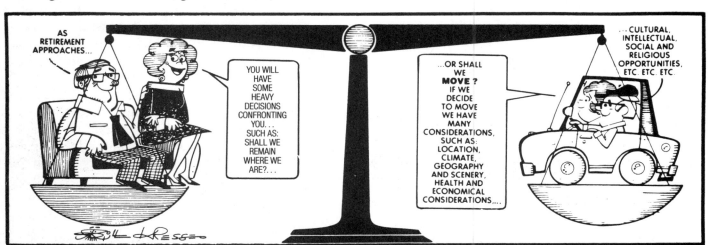

WHAT DO YOU PLAN TO DO?

There are a number of options open to you. What you choose will depend upon your own circumstances, needs and preferences. Your health may indicate that you should move to a milder climate. Your plans for leisure time activities may make you move closer to nature, or keep you close to the cultural offerings of the larger cities.

CHECK THE FEATURES BELOW WHICH ARE IMPORTANT TO YOU IN DETERMINING THE KIND OF HOUSING YOU NEED:

_____ Climate

_____ Distance from family

_____ Cost of moving

_____ Transportation facilities available

_____ Police and fire protection

_____ Streets, sidewalks, utilities near housing

_____ Shopping facilities nearby

_____ Taxes

_____ Place of worship nearby

_____ Physical limitations of family members

_____ Types of recreational facilities available

_____ Availability of employment

_____ Cost

_____ Safety of neighborhood

_____ Individual preference regarding isolation

_____ Good hospital nearby

A booklet, *Staying at Home: A Guide to Long Term Care and Housing,* discusses the types of housing and care that are available nationwide. For a free copy, ask for publication D14986 from: AARP, Fulfillment, 601 E Street, NW, Washington, DC 20049.

MOST THINK OF MOVING — BUT STAY PUT

The majority of those retiring say that they have given "some thought" to relocating. However, most stay where they are.

Studies indicate that only 20% to 25% of those who retire move away from their home communities within the first few years of retirement. Most who do move stay in the same state. Perhaps no more than 5% move to other states and other parts of the country.

Of the 75% to 80% who remain in their home communities, a substantial number do move to smaller homes or apartments or to other neighborhoods.

Despite all the advertising lures to "the rich possibilities for long healthy, rewarding retirement" in Sunbelt communities, the majority of retirees are not pulling up their deep roots in home areas to move away.

Certainly, Florida is full of retirees. So are Arizona and other areas away from snow and cold. So is North Carolina, an "in" state for many retiring today. Still, the numbers moving into Sunbelt—or Retirement Belt—states are a relatively low percentage of those retiring.

Why do most stay where they are? It's not simply inertia. Many are too closely tied to homes to move away. They value the memories. They want to remain near friends and neighbors, to stay in their churches, clubs and organizations with people they know, to do business with banks and stores they are accustomed to. In a nutshell, they want to continue living as much as possible as they did before retirement.

In thinking about where you will live in retirement, it is a good idea to begin with thinking about where you are living now. Why did you choose your present home? What are its advantages? Its disadvantages?

Did you make sacrifices in order to be convenient to your job or, perhaps, your spouse's job? To be near schools, no longer an advantage now that children are grown? To have a lot of space you no longer need, or perhaps a larger yard for the children, somewhat of a liability now?

Think also of what you might gain—and give up—by moving into a smaller home requiring less care, inside and outdoors, and costing less for utilities and perhaps for taxes.

Your options are to stay where you are, to move to a smaller place that might better meet your needs in older years without tearing up community roots, or to consider moving elsewhere.

CHECKLIST FOR LIVING

(Yes) (No)

❑   ❑   Is my present house suitable for Retirement living?

❑   ❑   Can my present house be remodeled for satisfactory Retirement living?

❑   ❑   Will I be able to handle the upkeep and maintenance of the house?s

❑   ❑   Will the costs of taxes and insurance be in my budget?

❑   ❑   Can my house be converted to a two-family house to rent?

❑   ❑   Have I checked the zoning?

❑   ❑   Have I considered using my home equity for income?*

❑   ❑   Is my present neighborhood safe?

❑   ❑   Have I checked the security of my house?

❑   ❑   Have I planned how to spend my time?

❑   ❑   Am I active in my Community?

❑   ❑   Are my friends important to me?

❑   ❑   Is it important to be near my family?

❑   ❑   Do I want to keep working after I retire?

❑   ❑   Do I want to stay where I'm known?

❑   ❑   Do I want to make a fresh start somewhere else?

❑   ❑   Before I move to a new area, have I experienced its different seasons?

❑   ❑   Is it close to shopping and public transportation?

❑   ❑   Is it near good medical care?

* BE VERY CAREFUL - GET SOME LEGAL AND FINANCIAL ADVICE.

THINGS TO CONSIDER IF YOU THINK OF RELOCATING

If you have considered staying in your present community and decided against it, go slow about making a final commitment.

A decision to relocate is, almost invariably, irreversible. Moving is physically and psychologically difficult—and it is an expensive drain on retirement resources.

Be absolutely sure of whatever decision you make.

Here are some things to consider:

● An area's climate, geography and scenery. No place offers a perfect year-round climate: Florida's promised winter warmth turns into hot and humid discomfort. If you enjoy changing seasons, the sameness of Florida seasons will very quickly become palling. If you're accustomed to mountains, hills and rolling country, the flatness in plains states will make you homesick. It's a good idea to visit a location you're interested in at different times of the year—and to stay long enough to recognize the flaws along with the advantages.

● The area's health advantages and facilities. Many retirees who decide to relocate do so for health reasons. Respiratory, coronary and rheumatic conditions might be relieved by settling in the right place—or can be aggravated by a wrong choice. Don't make a decision to relocate without consulting your doctor. And check on the availability of doctors and hospitals or clinics wherever you go. Don't take for granted that emergency help will be available.

● The area's economic advantages. Check the cost of living in any area in which you want to locate. It's a good idea to subscribe to a local newspaper and read it carefully to learn about prices (check the ads) and business activity. If you want to augment your income in retirement, are there job opportunities? Want ads might tell this but you probably will have to check the Chamber of Commerce or a Senior Citizen Agency. Remember that if you save money on clothing, heating and housing costs in Sunbelt areas, the savings may be partially offset by air conditioning costs during most of the year.

● Its religious and social opportunities. Make sure that you can continue to enjoy the kind of religious and social life you have had before. Are the facilities available? Generally, they are almost everywhere, but be sure. The same advice goes for recreational and sports possibilities, and for hobbies. The congeniality you find in religious, social recreational, sports and hobby groups is important to your happiness in a new home.

● Its cultural and intellectual advantages. Many communities that are desirable places to live in are limited in cultural and intellectual opportunities. You might not be able to take continuing education courses, enter Great Books discussion groups, hear good live performances of plays, music or the dance, or browse through museums. If these are things you enjoy, perhaps you'd better look for a college town offering these and all the other advantages you're seeking in a retirement home.

● The location and accessibility of the area. Shopping centers, restaurants, libraries, theaters, post offices, and other everyday facilities you might want are easily accessible almost everywhere now. Certainly you'll have no problems if you have a car. Still, check. Also, don't forget to look into the accessibility of airports offering adequate flight service if you might want to or have to travel by air. And is there train service? What about buses?

● Personal relationships. If you have no friends or relatives in the place you'd like to call your retirement home, visit there enough times to be sure the residents are congenial. Almost always they will be, but "outsiders" find it hard to break through barriers in a few places. The lack of quick friendliness and total acceptance in a community creates additional strain at a time when tearing up roots in one place and trying to set them in another is traumatic enough.

In a nutshell: Organize your thinking when you consider moving: Decide what you want and need in a new home, check carefully rather than deciding on a basis of retirement community ads or sunshine when you've just left winter snow, and do it at different times of the year. Summer vacations could be a start, but take time off later to sample other seasons.

Be over-cautious rather than sorry when it's too late.

There is a good test of how happy and well adjusted a retiree will be in a new retirement home.

How happy and how well adjusted are you in your present community?

If you are happy, active, a part of the community, enjoying its advantages and helping to serve its needs, there is almost no doubt that you can be as happy and adjusted in a new community.

If you have never become a part of your community, arguing that you are too busy and just not interested, don't expect anything better if you relocate.

When you go into a new community aggressively, don't wait to be invited to church, service or other clubs, or to participate in activities generally. Introduce yourself, mention what you were interested in before and say, "I'd like to be a part of things here."

You won't lack friends or a busy and useful life.

If you decide to relocate, the success of your move in the long run will be up to you.

LIVE WITH RELATIVES

Health factors may combine with economic ones to make living with children a necessity. The need for privacy suggests that even in these conditions, measures should be taken to avoid the unnecessary stress that can occur when two independent family units are forced into close association. It will require tact, maturity, and considerable caring on the part of family members to survive such forced intimacy without a deterioration of relationships.

There should be an understanding about roles in the family, and the older members of the household should share in the responsibilities of running the home. They should be given something constructive to do.

Where possible, private living room, bedroom, and bath facilities will enable the individual to have an independence which will be important for their (his or her) self-respect. Efforts should be made to encourage the family member to maintain a schedule of activities which is independent of the activities of the family. Their sense of identity should not be limited to their relationship to the family. They have interests and friendships which should be cultivated apart from their participation in the activities of the home.

The 1987 tax code includes a provision that allows you, at any age, to postpone the tax on the profit from a sale of your home if you buy another principal residence within a two-year period.

You become eligible for another tax break after you reach 55. You will pay no taxes on up to $125,000 (including deferred gain from the prior sale of a home or homes) of gain on the sale of your residence. This applies whether you buy a new home or not.

To be eligible you must have lived in the home for three of the last five years prior to the date of sale. Check with the IRS for details or ask for the latest edition of their publication "Tax Benefits for Older Americans."

Remember, these exclusions are once in a lifetime offers. If either you or your spouse have previously elected to exclude the gain you are not eligible to do so again.

TAKE A HOME REPAIR COURSE

Keep Up To Date

CHECKLIST FOR SAFETY

(Yes)	(No)	
☐	☐	No-slip tape in your bathtub or shower.
☐	☐	Grab bars and hand grips in shower, bathtubs and near toilets.
☐	☐	Can your towel bars and soap holders withstand sudden pulls?
☐	☐	Keep throw rugs away from top and bottom of stairs
☐	☐	Do all rugs have no-slip mats under them?
☐	☐	Do not wear loose-fitting slippers or bathrobes.
☐	☐	Are all chairs and stairs sturdy and free of wobbles?
☐	☐	Replace all frayed cords and broken plugs.
☐	☐	Relocate all furniture, lamp cords and clutter from traffic paths.
☐	☐	Do not run extension cords under rugs or carpets.
☐	☐	Avoid using space heaters, if possible. If they are necessary, keep away from flammable materials and out of traffic lanes.
☐	☐	No smoking while lying down.
☐	☐	Install smoke detectors and heat detectors throughout the house.
☐	☐	Install fire extinguishers near kitchen and work room.
☐	☐	Have escape routes planned from all areas of home in case of fire.
☐	☐	Avoid overloading one socket with several plugs.
☐	☐	Discard heavy, hard to handle, broken cooking utensils.
☐	☐	Are there handrails on all stairs and inclines?
☐	☐	Install night lights in the bedroom, bathroom and hallways.
☐	☐	Make sure stairways and other areas are well lighted.
☐	☐	If you live alone, have a friend or relative check in with you at regular intervals.
☐	☐	Keep first aid kit handy. Take first aid course, CPR course. Place emergency phone numbers near phone.

EARN SOME MONEY IN RETIREMENT

"Growing old is no more than a bad habit which a busy man has no time to learn." **ANDRE MAUROIS**

Do you have to work after retirement? Many people who could answer "no" to this question from a purely economic point of view, would have to say "yes" from a psychological one. There are other compulsions than not having enough income to live comfortably. Some people must work because of the additional rewards which work affords. Some must work to have an identity.

"What do you do?" is translated by some into the question, "Who are you?" Not having a job is almost like not being anybody. I am what I do. We have looked at this problem in our discussion about leisure. You are more than your job, but some people find in some kind of employment the activity which keeps them from learning the bad habit of growing old which Andre Maurois described in the introduction.

(To work and receive Social Security see Chapter 3.)

MUST I? MAY I?

The question for many is decided in terms of economic necessity. The choice is limited; work is essential for adequate income. The other question is, given that I wish to work, will I be able to find a job? Who will be interested in having an individual who has been retired from active work? How can I compete with the younger worker in terms of strength, ability to learn, contribution to the company?

There is a strong indication that given a choice, most older workers would prefer continuing with some kind of employment. There is a contribution which work makes to our lives which is not easily replaced by anything else. What, other than work, can give the following satisfactions to life?

- It is the basis for self-respect, for feeling that you are somebody who has something to contribute.
- It is a source of prestige and recognition. People appreciate your ability to perform.
- It provides a place for social participation. How many of your friendships are related to the job?
- It is a source of enjoyment, a chance to be creative.
- It is a way of helping others.
- It helps give order to the day, making time pass. You don't have to plan for or organize a great part of the day.
- It provides (in some cases) physical exercise and new experiences which take one out of the home.

THE ENEMY IS US

The greatest obstacle to your finding employment is the attitude which you have about yourself. To turn a familiar phrase, "we have nothing to fear but fear itself."

It's true that there are a number of myths which are going around about older workers. But there are some strong points which older workers have which can be emphasized. You can focus on the positive things which you have to offer, or you can show your prospective employer that you believe the myths that older workers are a poor risk.

The Department of Labor and other agencies have studied the performance of older workers and have come up with the following facts that refute the claims of myths about older workers:

CHANGES IN THE LAW THAT WILL AFFECT YOU!

END OF MANDATORY RETIREMENT AT AGE 70

WE CAN WORK... ...AS LONG AS WE LIKE!

Earning Money

Myth: "Older workers are too slow. They can't meet the production requirements."

● **Fact**: There is no significant drop in performance and productivity in older workers. Many older workers exceed the average output of younger employees.

Myth: "Older workers can't meet the physical demands of jobs."

● **Fact**: Fourteen percent of today's jobs require great strength and heavy lifting. Labor-saving machinery makes it possible for older workers to handle eighty-six percent of modern jobs without difficulty.

Myth: "Older workers are absent from work too often."

● **Fact**: The attendance record of workers over 65 compares favorably with that of other age groups.

Myth: "Older workers are inflexible. They're hard to train because they can't accept change."

● **Fact**: Adaptability depends on the individual, rather than on his age. Some young people are set in their ways, while a high proportion of older workers show flexibility in accepting a change in occupation and earnings.

Myth: "Hiring older workers increases our pensions and insurance costs."

● **Fact**: Most pension plans provide for benefits related to length of service or earnings, or both. Small additional pension costs, when incurred, are more than offset by the older worker's experience, lower turnover, and quality of work. Studies show the costs of group life, accident, and health insurance and workmen's compensation are not materially increased by hiring older workers.

The following check list contains favorable and unfavorable attitudes of older workers. Which ones apply to you?

_____ Has defeatist attitude toward getting work and difficult time impressing an employer favorably.

_____ Has stability which comes with maturity.

_____ Wastes less time on job than younger worker.

_____ Feels he is slowing down, and talks about this feeling with prospective employer.

_____ Has forgotten how to go about getting a job.

_____ Has less absenteeism and is more apt to stay on the job.

_____ Has safe work habits.

_____ Is reluctant to change occupations even though there is no work available in line with his previous type of work.

_____ Refuses to consider jobs paying less or having less prestige than former jobs because of personal pride.

_____ Has difficult time making a realistic evaluation of his limitations. Makes unrealistic demands as to wages, location, working conditions, etc.

_____ Has greater sense of responsibility.

_____ Has steady work habits and serious attitude toward job.

_____ Has a good appearance.

_____ Requires less supervision on job, once he is oriented.

_____ Tends to undersell himself and fails to impress prospective employers favorably.

_____ Is less distracted by outside interests, has less domestic troubles, and is capable of greater concentration.

AMERICANS AT WORK					
Age group	Percentage of men employed full-time	Percentage of women employed full-time	Age group	Percentage of men employed full-time or part-time	Percentage of women employed full-time or part-time
45 to 54	82.8	47.2	60 and 61	65.7	38.6
55 to 59	71.0	35.3	62 to 64	44.3	27.7
60 to 64	46.1	21.7	65 to 69	23.6	13.0
65 and older	8.2	2.7	70 and older	10.3	4.2

Source: Bureau of Labor Statistics.

IF YOU HAD YOUR DRUTHERS ...

If you had the job of matching the interests, skills, experience, and situation of a person like yourself to a job, what kind of employment would you select? Maybe you need to look at all of these factors to get a total picture. You may be interested in doing something you have little experience in doing. You may not like the kind of thing in which you have experience. Try "brainstorming" with your answers to the following questions:

Past Jobs Held
What did you like and dislike?
Skills and Abilities
What can you do best?
Educational Qualifications
Have you had special instruction?
Physical Limitations
Does your health rule out some jobs?
Goals
What would be ideal for you?

YOUR EXPERIENCE INVENTORY

Employment Objective. (As clearly and concisely as possible, indicate what you want to do.)

_____

_____

Employment History. (List employment in reverse chronological order.)

Dates		Job Title	Company Name
From	To	(Briefly State Your Duties)	Location
_____	_____	_____	_____
_____	_____	_____	_____
_____	_____	_____	_____
_____	_____	_____	_____

Miscellaneous Employment. (List part-time and/or minor employments, if you think these would help you, if not, skip this part.)

_____

_____

Education. (List schools in reverse chronological order.)

Dates		Name of School	Last Grade Completeted
From	To	and Location	Diploma, Degree and Major/Minor Subject
_____	_____	_____	_____
_____	_____	_____	_____
_____	_____	_____	_____
_____	_____	_____	_____

Additional Education. (List correspondence schools, company courses, armed forces schools, seminars, home study courses, adult school courses, etc.)

_____

_____

Professional Associations. (List organizations, clubs and other professional groups to which you belong or did belong.)

_____

_____

Interests. (List hobbies or volunteer activities, especially if they relate to the job you are applying for.)

_____

_____

THE JOB INTERVIEW

If you decide that you want to work for somebody else, you will usually have to talk to a representative of that company before you are employed. In the job interview you have a few minutes to tell about your qualifications. You will likely be talking to someone younger than yourself. You may be applying for a job which pays less than what you earned before retirement. Are you confident enough about yourself to avoid feeling defensive? Will your pride allow you to discuss your skills and experience realistically? Can you face the prospects of not receiving a job without feeling rejected as a person?

However you chose to answer the preceding questions you will find the interview more likely to result in a favorable impression on your part if you can:

- Stress your skills, not your limitations.
- Be poised and confident, but not cocky.
- Be pleasant but business-like.
- Speak firmly and clearly.
- Listen attentively to your interviewer's questions.
- Answer briefly and honestly.
- Stress your stability and good attendance record.
- Ask intelligent questions about the nature of the job.
- Be realistic if asked about your salary requirements.
- Leave when the interview is over, thanking the employer for the opportunity.

Poor impressions are left by those who ...

- are timid and ill at ease.
- are stubborn and argumentative.
- stress their need for a job.
- emphasize their age or personal problems.
- exaggerate their skills.
- criticize a former employer.
- talk too long.
- discuss salary, benefits, and hours before the employer brings up the subjects.
- show reluctance to fill out an application form, give references, or take a physical exam if requested.

HELP!

There are sources of help in locating a job or developing the skills needed to get one. They are:

1. Friends, relatives, former co-workers, or members of your group can be helpful. Tell them that you're looking for a job; and ask them for help in finding one.
2. Want ads in newspapers, professional journals, and trade magazines.
3. Industrial and craft unions.
4. U.S. Office of Personnel Management.
5. Private employment agencies (some charge the applicant a fee, and others collect the fee from the employer).
6. Yellow pages of telephone directory, industrial directories, Chamber of Commerce lists.
7. Professional associations.
8. Forty-Plus Clubs for executives in major cities.
9. Retired Officers Association (for members) 201 N. Washington St., Alexandria, VA 22314-2539.
10. Personnel offices.
11. College placement offices.
12. The library.
13. Nonprofit employment agencies. Your local Chamber of Commerce, and YMCA, Salvation Army, and your state employment agency should be able to tell you if there are agencies in your area.

SECOND CAREERS: TODAY'S JOB MARKET

In today's job market, with plant down-sizing, early retirement, and company mergers, many find themselves at a relatively early age looking for a new job or a new career. This is a marked change from the stability of employment many enjoyed ten and twenty years ago. Millions of American have and will be affected by this change.

What to do? While still working, continually develop your skills either at work, at your local adult educational center, community college, or university. Take courses that interest you and in subject areas where job possibilities could develop.

There are positive factors. You have work skills and experience. Older workers are needed almost everywhere.

Take an inventory of your talents.

List your goals, what you've always wanted to do, what you would enjoy doing.

Where in your area are your skills needed?

Volunteering can open job possibilities.

Check lists for job opportunities:

- Your local business association membership directory.
- Current/former co-workers, past employers.
- Friends and relatives and members of any group you belong to, church, community or fraternal.
- Placement officers, college, professional, and trade.
- Find out what businesses are expanding in your area.

NOTE: OVER 75% OF ALL JOBS ARE NEVER LISTED IN NEWSPAPERS OR PUBLIC EMPLOYMENT AGENCIES.

WORKING FOR SELF AND OTHERS

If you want to have a good job interview with a person you really like, and have your resume read by admiring and sympathetic eyes, try making an application to YOURSELF for a job! You can work out the hours which are agreeable to employer and employee, and there will never be a discussion over wages. Some retired persons will want to consider being their own boss, and there are many ways that this can be done ... some of them good.

WORKING FOR YOURSELF

Operating a part-time business may be your answer to the need to supplement your income and find meaningful ways to invest your time. If it is done on a small scale, it may not require as much capital and know-how as you would imagine. Considerable caution should be exercised, however, in the selection of a business. Figures vary but indicate that your chances of remaining three years in your business are about 50-50. Dun and Bradstreet ran a survey which revealed that 90% of such business failures were due to inexperience and incompetence.

This is the age of the chain and the corporation. Your choice of a business should not lead you into competition with such tough competitors. Check a regional office of the Small Business Administration for advice and information about opening a business, or write to: Small Business Administration, 409 3rd Street, SW, Washington, DC 20416.

Try to get an early start preparing for the business you will operate in retirement. You will need all the time you can get to familiarize yourself with the business, accumulate the capital needed for the investment, and purchase equipment needed before attempting to live on a retirement budget.

WHAT A WORKER OVER AGE 65 IN 1995 NETS FROM A JOB

Employment Income (Annual)	$12,000.00	$20,000.00	$30,000.00
Reduction in Social Security benefits	240.00	2,906.00	6,240.00
Social Security tax (FICA)	918.00	1,530.00	2,295.00
Additional federal/state taxes (estimated)	1,800.00	3,000.00	4,500.00
Job expenses (travel, lunch, etc.) (estimated)	3,000.00	3,000.00	3,000.00
Net Earnings	**6,042.00**	**9,564.00**	**13,965.00**
Monthly (Net) Earnings	**503.50**	**797.00**	**1,163.00**

Note: You may earn up to 11,280 per year in 1995 without losing any Social Security benefits. Starting at age 70, you may earn an unlimited amount and not lose benefits.

FINDING YOUR BUSINESS

Answering the questions listed below should give you some insights into the type of business which would suit your preferences.

- How well do I get along with other people?
- Am I ready to assume responsibility for payroll and business obligations?
- Do I like the proposed business enough to sacrifice for it?
- Am I prepared to take the risk involved in owning a business?
- Do I like to sell?
- Can I make decisions and live with them?
- How do I react to emergencies?
- Am I a good organizer?

The U.S. Small Business Administration lists 10 characteristics that a businessman should have. Rank yourself from 1 (exceptional), 2 (above average), 3 (average), 4 (below average), to 5 (deficient) to get your businessman's profile.

Trait	Rank
Initiative	_____
Positive attitude	_____
Leadership ability	_____
Organizing ability	_____
Industry	_____
Responsibility	_____
Quick and accurate judgments	_____
Sincerity	_____
Perseverance	_____
High level of energy	_____

The more "1's" and "2's" you have listed, the easier it will be for you to adjust to running a business.

Considering the high mortality rate of business and the possibilities of over-extending yourself in demands on your money, health and time, get plenty of information, and be sure that you know what you need to have done in going into business.

The Usefulness of a Business Plan

If you wish to start your own business, preparing a good business plan is the first step. If you need finance, or even if you only want to bring your bank manager on board in case you run into problems later on, you'll need a business plan. Having a thorough one demonstrates that you are a self-starter who has put a great deal of thought into your business idea.

Aside from money matters, a business plan will help your overall management of your new enterprise. Getting the business plan right can mean the difference between success and failure.

What does a good business plan look like? Each business plan is different, but, in general, it should include a description of the business including short- and long-term goals, an analysis of the market being entered (including a discussion of competitors' strengths and weaknesses and your competitive advantage), and financial details including start-up costs, the size of the investment required and profit and cash-flow projections for a minimum of one year ahead.

WHEN CONSIDERING A SECOND CAREER...
1- KNOW WHAT YOU WANT FROM YOUR NEW CAREER
2- TAKE INVENTORY OF YOUR TALENTS, AND DREAMS
3- ENJOY EXPLORING 2nd CAREER OPTIONS
4- LEARN A NEW CAREER, JOB OR SKILL
5- HOW ABOUT STARTING YOUR OWN BUSINESS?

WORKING AT HOME

Having your business where you live—more than 40 million Americans work out of their homes—eliminates some of the problems of working at a separate location. You do not have to worry about paying rent for the business, nor do you have to incur transportation costs getting to and from work. It will also be easier to maintain a schedule that is more relaxed if you are working out of your own home.

One warning, though: Check out any zoning regulations or licensing procedures that you might have to comply with that apply to businesses in private homes.

FRANCHISES

This is the kind of business venture which has some of the features of owning your own business and some of the features of working for somebody else. You have to put up some capital, but often the national organization has standards and methods of operation which are part of your obligation to the jointly-owned business. The organization often will assume responsibility for giving you training, and will supervise the market so that no unfair competition will arise from another member of the same organization.

Franchises are really a form of licensing. The franchisor, which is usually an owner, service, product or method, distributes through affiliated dealers who are the franchises. If you purchase a franchise, often you will be given exclusive rights to the area served by your franchise. But you can still run into trouble from other companies offering similar franchises, so be careful to check beforehand for competition in the area you want a franchise.

Each franchise should be carefully investigated before the decision is made to invest in it. Many fraudulent promoters are at work in the field offering schemes which are little more than obligations on the part of the "victims" to purchase supplies or goods from the promoters. Ample advice is available from Better Business Bureau, Chambers of Commerce, and others, so that no individual need stumble into a venture without adequate information.

WORKING FOR OTHERS

Look at the chapter on volunteering to share your time with others. There are jobs which are directly related to service for others, and the compensation is a combination of a modest pay check and the knowledge that you have made life a more rewarding experience for someone else. These jobs take as much of your time as you care to give.

BE PREPARED

If you are seriously interested in developing the skills necessary to go back to work or start your own business, two of the best places to go for information and help are your public library and your local college.

Library shelves many times have sections on employment and retirement, and either category might have the facts and advice you're looking for.

Colleges, particularly Junior and Community Colleges, also provide services for those whose sights are set on the job market. In addition to courses which can develop skills and expertise in specific areas (such as Business, Accounting, or Education), many colleges offer classes designed for adults who wish to know more about developing second careers and getting back into the mainstream of employment. Check with your local two-year college for details of their programs.

BOOKS THAT COULD BE HELPFUL

The Quick Job-Hunting Map. Richard Bolles. 1990. ISBN# 1-89815-387-5. $3.95 plus $3.50 handling. Workbook also available, ISBN# 1-89815-152-X. 1985 rev. ed. $2.50 plus $1.00.

What Color Is Your Parachute & Practical Manual for Job Hunters & Career Changers. Richard Bolles. 1995. ISBN# 1-89815-633-5. $14.95 plus $3.50 handling.

How to Paint a Picture of Your Ideal Job. Richard Bolles. 1993. ISBN# 1-89815-307-7. $7.95 plus $3.50 handling.

You can order these books from: Ten Speed Press, P.O. Box 7123, Berkeley, CA 94707.

MYTH

"A perpetual holiday is a good working definition of hell." —**GEORGE BERNARD SHAW**

"All animals except man know that the chief business of life is to enjoy it." —**SAMUEL BUTLER**

"Success or failure in the second forty years, measured in terms of happiness, is determined more by how we use or abuse our leisure than any any other factor ... a super abundance of leisure, or the abuse thereof has marked and initiated the decadence of cultures throughout history."
—**DR. EDWARD J. STIEGLITZ,** The Second Forty Years.

Retirement should be a transition from toil t leisure. It should see a transfer of the energies w formerly devoted to making a living to the ne business of living well. In the transition you wi have to reallocate your time.

- Will your leisure be the perpetual holiday mentioned by Shaw, or the time when you discover how to enjoy life as never before?

- Will your use of leisure time result in success or failure in your attempt to achieve happiness during retirement?

- How much leisure time will you have on your hands, and how difficult will your schedule be after full-time employment no longer accounts for the major part of your daytime activities? What will replace the satisfactions that work has afforded?

The consideration of the above questions will lead you into an examination of yourself ... who you really are ... what you really want ... what your attitude is toward the use of your time. This chapter will provide you with an opportunity to look at yourself and to consider the alternatives open to you for structuring your time.

You'll explore what adjustments may be necessary to meet your basic human needs as you attempt to fill your life with meaning that is not derived specifically from the "work ethic" on which our country was founded.

HOW MUCH ... AND WHAT KIND OF TIME:

As you look toward having nothing to do, thi seems very appealing after so many years of hav ing too little "free time." If you look forward t "doing nothing," plan to do a lot of that ... for few weeks. And fishing? ... and traveling? ... an just sitting in the rocking chair? ... Yes, all o those things ... for a short time.

Remember, however, that the reason they seer so appealing is that you have had little opportunit to do them. A vacation is a vacation because comes infrequently, but a vacation EVERY DA OF THE YEAR? That's something else agair Remember to build quality into the hours you hav for leisure.

Unplanned time leads to boredom, a feeling o guilt, and a sense of frustration. As strange as may seem, these factors have caused many peopl to prefer working even when it is not an economi necessity for them to do so.

A recent study at Duke University's Center o Aging revealed that over half of the 200 men sur veyed (52%) said they got more satisfaction from work than they did from leisure. Fifty-five percen of the 200 women surveyed said they enjoye working more than they did having free time.

"HAVE YOU CONSIDERED **REPAIRMAN?**"

CAN YOU ACCEPT LEISURE?

You need to decide whether or not you can accept the free time you have earned for yourself. We can be misers with our time just as much as the individual who can put money away but is unable to spend it.

We have had little preparation for leisure. Walter Kerr, in *The Decline of Pleasure*, notes that "the twentieth century has relieved us of much labor without at the same time relieving us of the conviction that only labor is meaningful." It may be that to really enjoy leisure you will have to "learn not to work." You may have to teach yourself that it is right for you to enjoy doing something for the pleasure it brings, without having to prove that it serves any higher purpose. You may have to retrain your mind to accept that leisure is not "inactivity," and that non-work activities may be as necessary and "useful" as those for which we formerly received our paychecks.

The goal in retirement is not just to fill your time, but to fill it in a meaningful way. "Free time" is what you have when you are allowed to determine what you will do without outside coercion.

"Leisure" is the term we apply to those activities with which we fill our "free time." The kind of leisure which we will be able to "accept" has the following characteristics:

- We do it because we want to.
- We anticipate it with pleasure and remember it fondly.
- We may do it alone, or with others.
- We feel good about it, physically and mentally.
- It contributes to others, as well as to ourselves.
- We may do it for fun, or we may do it for profit.

The correct use of leisure can affect our health and our wealth. We can lose both if our bodies and our minds are wasted through inactivity, or in useless occupation.

> *An aging individual, by aimless living, can accelerate his deterioration as he grows older. The older the individual, the greater is the need for an all-absorbing motive, an interest in life. At 55 or 60 or 65, instead of receding from the useful stream of meaningful activities, he should establish new interests, or a second career.*
> — **DR. EDWARD L. BORTZ**

Learn to accept leisure. Work if you wish, and be as active in your retirement as you care to be, but accept the fact that it's OK to enjoy many different activities, including that activity of doing nothing.

WHAT LEISURE ACTIVITIES CONTRIBUTE TO YOUR LIFE

What you do with your time must be more than being busy. Providing activity which neglects the personality and the person is like throwing a life buoy to a drowning person; it keeps his head above the water, but doesn't really rescue him.

Demand that your efforts be rewarded. Don't settle for filling time! Those activities which are worth your time should ...

- Create excitement,
- Stimulate your emotions and give you a new zest,
- Be both physically and intellectually stimulating.

It's a good idea to have your spouse ponder over the same categories—then compare your impressions, and see what things you have in common to explore together in retirement!

There are some basic needs which remain constant throughout life, and many of these can be met through a wise selection of leisure activities.

Would you like to look at some of these basic needs and see how they compare to your present choices of leisure activities? List alongside the corresponding need the activity which you are presently engaged in which makes a contribution to that need. In the right-hand column, list additional activities which you would like to consider in the future to meet that need.

Need	Present Activities	Projected Activities
Recognition		
Entertainment		
Self-expression, creativity		
Participation, belonging		
Adventure, new experience		
Learning		
Security		
Physical fitness		
Contemplation		
Self-growth		
Usefulness		
Income		

CRITERIA FOR SELECTION OF AN ACTIVITY

If you like an activity, that is one good reason for considering it, but there are other factors which you may want to consider. Some activities which have brought satisfaction to others have been found to have these qualities:

1. A beginner can attain a sense of accomplishment.

2. Basic skills can be mastered readily.

3. Real proficiency can come with practice.

4. It has so many facets that it doesn't become tiresome.

5. It is within your budget.

6. It enlarges a skill you already possess.

7. It offers opportunity for self-development.

8. It provides a change of pace from your routine.

9. It can be practiced all year long.

10. It represents a blend of several activities.

11. It can be pursued in spite of some physical limitations.

12. It puts you in touch with other people.

13. It provides challenges to improve or grow or become more proficient in an area of interest.

As you analyze who you are and what you expect from an activity, you probably can determine why it appeals to you in terms of your answers to the questions listed below. Look at the activities you have enjoyed and those you are considering and match them to the criteria developed from the questions listed on the next page.

CHECK LIST POSSIBILITIES

- ❏ Gardening
- ❏ Sewing
- ❏ Music
- ❏ Photography
- ❏ Acting
- ❏ Painting
- ❏ Crafts
- ❏ Collecting
- ❏ Writing
- ❏ Cooking
- ❏ Woodworking
- ❏ Repairing Things
- ❏ Community Projects
- ❏ Politics
- ❏ Religious
- ❏ Charitable Activities
- ❏ Club
- ❏ Family Activities
- ❏ Family Outings
- ❏ Entertaining
- ❏ Walking
- ❏ Swimming

- ❏ Camping
- ❏ Fishing
- ❏ Exercising
- ❏ Dancing
- ❏ Television
- ❏ Ham Radio
- ❏ Sport Events
- ❏ Time to be Alone
- ❏ Enjoying Nature
- ❏ Museums - Art Galleries
- ❏ Learning
- ❏ Reading
- ❏ Part Time Work
- ❏ Investing
- ❏ Bowling
- ❏ Boating
- ❏ Bicycling
- ❏ Little League
- ❏ Scout Master
- ❏ Take Courses
- ❏ Elderhostel
- ❏ Golf

START ENJOYING YOUR FAVORITE ACTIVITIES **NOW!**

..IN EARLY MORNING, TAKE A WALK,

STAY IN TOUCH WITH YOUNGER PEOPLE

PLAY GOLF,

PLAN YOUR ACTIVITIES AROUND A CERTAIN TIME OF THE DAY, AS EXAMPLES,,

HIKING TRAIL

PLAN SOME ACTIVITIES WITH FRIENDS

10. | VOLUNTEER

THE FIRST PERSON YOU HELP IS YOURSELF

"People who stay young do so because of an active interest that provides satisfaction through participation."— **DR. WILLIAM C. MENNINGER**

"Wherever a man turns, he can find someone who needs him. Even if it is a little thing, do something for which you get no pay but the privilege of doing it. For remember, you don't live in a world all your own. Your brothers are here, too."
— **DR. ALBERT SCHWEITZER**

"All who would win joy, must share it; happiness was born a twin."— **BYRON**

In the preceding chapter we looked at the amount of time you are going to have during retirement and suggested some possible uses for it. We suggested that you need to take a good look at yourself, and fill your time with experiences which bring pleasure to you. Relax, have a good time.

In this chapter we are asking you to do the same thing. Because of who you are, you probably won't be able to find continual happiness thinking about yourself. The human spirit is too great to be contented seeking the gratification of its own desires. Because of the sheer "fun" of sharing, many people feel a keen satisfaction in giving a part of themselves away in community service activities.

You must plan for meaningful uses of the free time you will have in retirement. A lack of planned time can lead to boredom, a feeling of guilt and a sense of frustration. Devote part of your time to what gives you personal pleasure, without worrying about the activity being practical or whether it serves a higher purpose: spend time with a hobby, sports, self-expression or creativity, the adventures of travel, further education or even just the entertainment of watching television, reading and listening to music. By work you have earned the right to enjoy leisure as you want to spend it. However, for your fullest satisfaction in retirement years, consider spending part of your free time in volunteer work with and for others. One out of every four adults in the United States does some volunteer work during each year. It might not be

much and it might not be for a long time but volunteer work does involve a sharing of personal time and interests and a participation with other toward a common objective.

SERVICE INSTEAD OF SALARY

You may not have decided to enter retirement without paid employment, but to the extent that your job responsibilities have lessened, your need for a replacement increases. You may not have realized the degree to which your sense of personal worth has been related to your job. During your early and middle years you have a definite (at times almost overwhelming) sense of responsibility. You are needed by family; you contribute to society through your work.

Community service activities now offer you such job-related satisfactions as:
● The comradeship of congenial people.
● A chance for recognition.
● An opportunity to contribute to a useful goal.
● An opportunity to belong to a worthwhile group.

You need to give of yourself more than the service organizations need to have your help. The principal beneficiary of your service is YOU.

There is really no way of counting all the things people do or the time they spend doing them—no way, for example, to total the hours devoted on Sundays alone to church work, even just the volunteer work of preparing for and teaching Sunday School classes. However, a recent Conference Board survey of 3,800 upper-echelon managers and professionals who retired from major U.S. corporations between 1961 and 1976 found that 11% were doing volunteer work while holding retirement jobs for pay and another 22% were working strictly as volunteers.

The point is, there's a need—often a very serious need—for every man or woman to serve, somewhere, as a volunteer worker. The extent of participation is up to the volunteer. It can be as little as an hour a week. It can be much more. It can be a minimum of personal involvement, with only assistance in routine chores, or it can be deeply personal.

Dr. Allen G. Brailey, a Boston physician noted the vital role which service plays in assuming the place formerly occupied by the job or the family. "Do not retire from work; retire to more congenial work for the Community Fund, for the Red Cross, for the church or the schools, for the Scouts." Someone has suggested that service to one's fellow man fills the need in the retired person which service to children and grandchildren formerly supplied.

WHAT SHARING DOES FOR YOU

If activities are carefully selected, someone has suggested that they can make the following contributions, most of which relate to your own personal well-being:

1. Lessen the shock of disengagement from work.
2. Delay senility.
3. Stimulate the mind and body, reducing health problems.
4. Combat the waste of human resources.
5. Enrich the community through volunteer services.
6. Give positive pleasure.

HOW YOU CAN CHOOSE THE BEST ACTIVITY FOR YOU

There are so many needs, you can afford to choose among them to find the one which suits what you have to offer. If you can begin early … even before you retire, this will give you a chance to practice. Some companies are beginning to allow their men approaching retirement to devote time before actual retirement to community service. This permits a gradual transfer of interest and skills to the service-oriented job as formal employment draws to a close.

Ask yourself the following questions when considering how to invest your time:
1. Is it something about which I care deeply?
2. Does it require a skill I possess?
3. Does it provide association with congenial people?
4. Does it require time I am prepared to give?
5. Do I enjoy fixing things (if that is required)?
6. Do I enjoy creating things (if that is required)?
7. Am I good at selling things (if that is required)?
8. Does it involve working with people or things? (Which do I prefer?)

INVENTORY OF INTERESTS AND SKILLS

Check the following resources that you have. Circle those which you do exceptionally well, or which you find exceptional satisfaction in sharing.

__Human concern
__Writing experience
__Growing things
__Caring for children
__Working with the handicapped
__Teaching skills
__Photography skills
__Political interests
__Library skills
__Cooking skills
__Organizing ability
__Playing a musical instrument
__Visiting skills
__Knowledge of athletics
__Others

__Typing facility
__Selling ideas
__Language skills
__Speaking skills
__Caring for older people
__Carpentry
__Nursing training
__Church interests
__Entertaining skills
__Supervisory skills
__Hunting skills
__Knowledge of legal matters
__Meeting people
__Bookkeeping skills

"GEORGE SAID HE'D LOVE TO BE A VOLUNTEER...
...BUT THERE'S NOT MUCH DEMAND FOR WHAT HE DOES BEST."

WHAT YOU HAVE: WHO NEEDS IT?

Nationwide, at least four and a half million persons age 65 or over are currently engaged in some type of volunteer work. If you are considering sharing your knowledge and experience through volunteer work, you can begin looking in your own neighborhood. Chances are, many groups in your area employ volunteer workers or are seeking their help.

After-school programs at your local school, church or synagogue, Salvation Army center or Y could be greatly expanded with your volunteer help. Many working parents are unable to be with their children until late in the afternoon. Volunteering to participate in constructive after-school programs not only benefits the children but yourself as well as you find an enjoyable and valuable way to contribute to the community.

Other ideas:

… Helping at your church or synagogue
… Providing transportation to the aged for shopping and visits to the doctor
… Conducting parties at shut-in centers
… Making tray favors for hospital patients
… Collecting and repairing clothing
… Assisting with public health programs
… Reading books to the sightless or ill
… Sponsoring Girl or Boy Scout troop
… Volunteering in city library
… Working in United Fund
… Cooperating with Friendly Visitors programs
… Volunteering for work in nursing homes
… Participating in telephone "reassurance service" for elderly
… Participating in "Meals on Wheels" program
… Assisting in building, repairing community playgrounds
… Peace Corps
… School volunteers
… Red Cross
… Literacy volunteers
… Big Brothers
… Big Sisters
… Little League

WHERE TO FIND WHERE HELP IS WANTED

Many communities have central bureaus to act a clearing houses for nonprofit agencies in need o volunteer help. Look in the telephone director under VOLUNTEER; COMMUNITY—Communit Chest, Community Service Council; EXTENSIO SERVICE (small towns and rural areas). Your loca library should also have listings of voluntee opportunities in the area.

Check with the social, civic and religiou groups represented in your community. They wi have projects and can refer you to additional ager cies which would welcome your participation.

How about politics? Check with your loca party representatives for suggestions about ho you can support candidates and issues you respec The League of Women Voters offers opportunitie for women to be informed and influential in th political arena.

How about supporting agencies which suppor you, as a retired person?

1. Does your community have a Council o Aging?
2. Are there organized groups of retired peopl in your area?

Are there programs presented by agencies an institutions which benefit the retired community These may include universities, community col leges, adult education classes, ETV programmin for the aging, churches, libraries, etc. Suppor these programs by becoming better informed an seeing that others know of the services offered b the agencies. The Points of Light Foundation is private clearinghouse providing information o local volunteer activities. For information write t Points of Light Fnd., Attn: Volunteer Informatio 1737 H Street, NW, Washington, DC 20006.

DISCOVER THE STRENGTH OF UNITED ACTION

Find out where retired people meet for concerte action and join others like yourself. Ideas wil emerge as you discuss your problems and you concerns. YOU CAN DO SOMETHING T HELP OTHERS AND TO HELP YOURSELF .. if you do not insist on working by yourself:

Visit your Senior Center, if you have one i your community. If you do not have a Senio Center, discuss with other adults how you ca organize one. It can be the center of meetings which will provide the satisfactions once afforded by your job. It can be the center from which community service ideas will originate. It can provide opportunity for that participation which keeps you young, and for that sharing which insures your joy.

VOLUNTEERING — WHEN TO BEGIN?

You do not have to wait for retirement to begin volunteer work. If you are still working, now is the time to engage yourself in voluntary service. You can start on a limited basis, as your time permits, and extend your service in retirement. The important thing is to develop now a way of channeling the extra time you will have in retirement.

In addition to making better use of your free time, there are other benefits to be derived from volunteer service. Such work often leads to new friendships, educational, cultural and social activities.

Your new friends and activities are especially important if you have not maintained outside interests during your working years. By starting volunteer work now, you will be going into retirement with an established circle of friends whose interests are similar to your own. Their companionship and the accompanying activities will help insure a smooth transaction into retirement.

Another plus for volunteer service—it is good work experience. If you are thinking about starting a part-time job or a second career when you retire, doing some volunteer work now in your area of interest can give you the background needed to reach your goal. Or if you are considering a certain line of work but have some doubts, volunteer service may be just the way to help you decide what you really want to do.

BOOKS THAT COULD BE HELPFUL

Volunteer! The Comprehensive Guide to Voluntary Service in the United States and Abroad. Marjorie Adoff Cohen. 1992-93. $8.95 plus $1.50 for handling. Order from: CIEE, 205 East 42nd Street, New York, NY 10017.

The Three Boxes of Life: And How to Get Out of Them. Richard N. Bolles. 1994. ISBN# 0-9-13-668-58-3. $15.95 plus $3.50 for handling. Order from: Ten Speed Press, P.O. Box 7123, Berkeley, CA 94707.

FOR AN EXCITING AND ENJOYABLE RETIREMENT

Perhaps it's time to think about school for yourself. Tens of thousands of others approaching 65 or who are already retired are attending classes this fall. A large majority are attending school part-time.

Today's trend is to sign up for classes that will make life and retirement more exciting and perhaps more profitable.

Of course, you don't have to go to college for a continuing education. Your purposes might be served as well if you take adult education courses available through your public school system or offered by one of the various organizations—perhaps your YMCA or YMHA—that sponsors courses.

If you have a lively mind and an interest in improving it, you almost certainly can find educational opportunities (often free or at a minimum charge) that can open up a world of vast horizons in your later years.

The sharpness of a mind generally is blunted—not by age—but by disuse. This can happen at any age.

Those reasonably healthy can maintain skills and abilities well into, and perhaps beyond, their 80's, and the ability to learn new things is also maintained. If mental responses are slowed a little, this is more than offset by the fact that the older you are, the greater your advantage in being able to apply to learning a background of knowledge and experience younger people have not acquired.

So—don't hold back. And don't feel that it's eccentric to go back to school, or shy away from being taught by a younger person.

Many now are interested in making up for years when going to school was not possible. Continuing education courses offer opportunities to take elementary and high school level equivalency courses, leading to diplomas. In some programs it is possible to obtain credit in "'life experiences"—in other words having your jobs and activities count toward a degree.

Check out your
Local Library
The Nearest College
Your Community Center
The Local YMCA/YMHA
The Board of Education

Explore the possibilities of the many course available that are intended to enrich the lives c adults in your community, or to prepare them fc better or different jobs during their workin years—or in retirement.

Some courses are considered to be cultura There are Great Books classes, history studie courses in art or music appreciation and histor others in current issues, politics, philosophy an similar subjects.

Some are practical. These often include incom management and investing, health, home and au repairs, legal and tax matters, sewing, cooking an the like. Courses like these can be invaluable du ing your retirement years, when money is tigh The skills you learn can not only give you person; satisfaction, but they can save you money—a re inflation fighter.

CULTURAL, PRACTICAL, HOBBIES, EMPLOYMENT COURSES

Other classes are hobby-oriented. Many contir uing education programs include courses in suc things as art, photography, crafts, golf, and othe sports. Hobby-oriented courses offer chances t explore ways to spend your retirement leisur enjoyably.

Many are directed toward present or future job Courses in bookkeeping, computer programmin; office skills, real estate, medical technology, ar the basics of starting your own business are avai able in most communities. Costs vary greatly, bi usually there is a Senior Citizen discount.

If you are among those who didn't go to colleg or complete college work toward a diploma, no is a good time to get started. Or if you are amor those with keen interests in any field, it's a goc time to satisfy them by looking through a colleg catalog and signing up for a course or two. TI range of classes is wider than in adult education programs sponsored by public school systems or local organizations, and the subject matters are probably more advanced.

Many colleges and universities run extension courses, also known as continuing education programs, in centers around the college area. Many are offered at night or during weekends. They may or may not be credit courses—that is, giving credits toward eventual college or university degrees. While the costs may be high, discounts are often given to those in their 60's or older.

To find out what is available and what the entrance requirements will be, you should contact the Dean of Admissions (or even the Dean of Older Students, a relatively new part of some institutions) at your local college or university. Some schools have the same requirements for older applicants that they have for younger ones, but many do not require a high school diploma for older applicants whose backgrounds suggest an aptitude for college level work.

If you take courses for credits, you will have to meet the same requirements as younger students: attending classes, doing assigned work, turning in papers, and taking tests and examinations. You also will be graded, but don't let that make you nervous—surveys show that older students rate as well as those in other age groups.

Those really interested in college may find "weekend college" programs in their area. Classes are scheduled on Saturdays and Sundays, usually lasting two or three hours instead of one to cover a whole week's work in a day. It's hard work but a good way to get a diploma.

All we have said applies also to Junior and Community Colleges, which may be more convenient than four-year schools to many who are interested in continuing educations. There are other points in their favor: the local two-year colleges are often free to older applicants, and ordinarily anyone who is interested can sign up without questions about high school backgrounds.

You may have heard about correspondence courses, either part of college extension programs or offered privately. These can be a good idea for independent learning, even though being in a class where questions are asked and comments are made is beneficial to the learning process and your enjoyment.

Be particularly careful when you see private organizations offer courses in computer programming, art, writing, and other subjects — often with promises of "sure" employment or income. Check with a Better Business Bureau before you sign up.

Many who are interested primarily in "recreational" improvement of minds pay too little attention to local libraries, museums, galleries, and even television as aids to a continuing education. Local institutions often sponsor lecture series or talks on topics of the day. These are mini-educational programs that tend to be interesting as well as informative.

TV offers much more than entertainment pro-

SOME REASONS TO RETURN TO SCHOOL

To seek knowledge for its own sake.

To share a common interest with my spouse or friend.

To become a more effective citizen.

To get relief from boredom.

To carry out the recommendation of some authority.

To satisfy an enquiring mind.

To overcome the frustration of day-to-day living.

To be accepted by others.

To supplement a narrow previous education.

To stop myself from becoming a "vegetable".

To maintain or improve my social position.

To escape an unhappy relationship.

To provide a contrast to my previous education.

To comply with the suggestions of someone else.

To learn just for the sake of learning.

To make new friends.

To improve my ability to participate in community work.

To acquire knowledge to help with other educational courses.

To fulfill a need for personal associations and friendships.

To participate in group activity.

To gain insight into my personal problems.

To help me earn a degree, diploma or certificate.

To escape television.

To prepare for community service.

To gain insight into human relations.

To have a few hours away from responsibilities.

To learn just for the joy of learning.

To become acquainted with congenial people.

To provide a contrast for the rest of my life.

To get a break in the routine of home or work.

To improve my ability to serve mankind.

To keep up with others.

To improve my social relationships.

grams. In many areas, courses in general education or university studies are worthwhile whether you sign up to receive course material and to have your work monitored, or whether you just audit the programs aired.

Well, now that you know more about what you can find in education, nothing should stop you from having a happier, more interesting retirement.

All it takes is a little more time, a little energy, and some motivation to get you started on the way to being a younger-feeling, more alive, and more stimulated person.

RETIREMENT: EARLIER OR LATER?

When should you retire? This is fast becoming the number one question on the minds of many American workers. Only a short time ago, the decision when to retire was probably not yours to make. But recent changes in the law and more flexible pension plans now give many workers exciting new retirement options.

What this means is that most American workers now have a broader choice to make when they try to pinpoint a retirement age. For many workers today, the time span is from 55 to 58 to 70—a 12 to 15 year period. With greater freedom in selecting a date for retirement, it is important that you choose carefully. As we shall see, retiring before or after the right time may lead to problems. The right choice will help to insure a successful retirement.

YOUR OPTIONS

You no longer are required to retire at 70. The 1986 amendments to the FEDERAL AGE DISCRIMINATION IN EMPLOYMENT ACT bars mandatory retirement except under a few specific circumstances (under certain conditions, companies may enforce mandatory retirement practices for policy-making executives). Now older workers must be assessed for continued employment solely on a basis of ability—not age. This means you have three options:

- You can retire voluntarily at 65, as before, and begin collecting Social Security.
- You can elect to stay on working.
- You can take early retirement. The liberalization of pension plans in recent years has resulted in a rise in retirement before 65. Others who are not covered by a pension plan may continue to work as long as possible.

SOCIAL SECURITY AND RETIREMENT AGE

Current Social Security law gradually increases the retirement age from 65 to 67 by the year 2027. The chart at right indicates the age at which you can retire and receive full benefits (see page 23 for a discussion of how your Social Security benefits will be affected by a decision to retire early).

RETIRE WHEN IT'S BEST FOR YOU

Whether or not you elect to stay on the job past retirement age, the option you choose must depend on your personal circumstances. You may want to quit earlier and take your pension and another, easier job. You may want to work on past 65 to meet continuing high costs for medical care, the children's college costs or other needs. Or you may be ready to quit at 65 to take life easier.

Whatever you do, whenever you retire, you must remember that you face psychological changes. Idleness may give you a feeling of guilt and shame, a loss of self-esteem, a withdrawal from society. It doesn't have to be that way. But it often is. In retirement you must face yourself

Age to Receive Full Social Security Benefits	
Year of Birth	**Full Retirement Age**
1937 or earlier	65
1938	65 and 2 months
1939	65 and 4 months
1940	65 and 6 months
1941	65 and 8 months
1942	65 and 10 months
1943-1954	66
1955	66 and 2 months
1956	66 and 4 months
1957	66 and 6 months
1958	66 and 8 months
1959	66 and 10 months
1960 and later	67

afresh. To keep free of self-pity and bitterness, you must accept your situation, compensate for whatever losses might come, and remind yourself that what is important is not what you've lost, but what you still have and still can do.

In short, you must learn to focus on retirement as a positive experience. Retirement is a new beginning; it gives you the chance to develop and expand your interests in ways that were not possible during your working years. Before retirement, much of your time is taken up by the day to day necessity of a working routine. In retirement, the end of that routine means the beginning of new opportunities. Make the most of this break!

EARLY RETIREMENT: AN EARLIER START ON A NEW LIFE

The trend toward earlier retirements is not only a result of the liberalized policies that make them possible; it is also a result of today's new and rosier image of retirement. Retirement no longer is considered to be the start of a person's Age of the Rocking Chair. Today's retiree can usually look forward to continued activity.

To those asking the question, should I retire early?, you should consider these questions:

Why? Retire early to what? Do you have a new life waiting for you?

For some workers, early retirement is not necessarily a free and happy choice. As many as one out of every five men who leave jobs before 65 do so because of their health or physical condition. A somewhat higher percentage of women retiring early cite such reasons.

If the work is getting too onerous, and particularly if doctors recommend taking things easier in your 50s or early 60s, then retiring may certainly be the thing to do.

However, most are still physically fit and able to continue on the job up to 65—and beyond that common retirement age. Those who are should consider carefully the pros and cons of early retirement, the possible rewards and the potential pitfalls. Those who have worked for three or four decades will find inactivity difficult. They must substitute something for work. They should have a carefully thought out new life ahead. While that is true for everyone who retires, regardless of their age, it is particularly true for those retiring early. Younger retirees must look ahead not for an average decade or two, as those 65 must, but as long as three decades.

So, if you're going to start a new life early, ask

yourself what is it going to be like? Early retirement is not for everyone: you must be ready for and able to take it in full stride and to enjoy most of all, you must be able to afford it, not just at the time of early retirement but through the years to come.

CAN YOU AFFORD TO RETIRE?

You should be well aware of the impact of inflation on those who retire. It is a problem now, and is likely to continue to be one. While the rate of inflation has fortunately been considerably reduced, it is still a factor; a four percent rate of inflation amounts to over a 20% rise in the cost of living in just five years.

Remember, dollars are worth less, year to year. It's hard to live with inflation while you're working. It will be even harder when you retire to live on fixed income. Costs go up and, except for cost-of-living changes in Social Security benefits, income of retirees may not keep up with living costs.

Retirement on a full pension and with full Social Security benefits is difficult in years of inflation. The problems will be considerably worse for those who elect to retire earlier with smaller pensions and Social Security payments. This is something you must keep in mind.

Unless you can retire early and build up your reserves through a new job, a new business or a new career, you will probably be better off economically to work longer and concentrate on accumulating reserves for a more secure future.

However, dollars are not the only thing to think about.

Work satisfaction is another important factor in making decisions about whether to continue on the job as long as you can or to retire early.

Sometimes it is better to have a simpler future with less income and not as much socked away than to spend additional years in a job that you dread going to.

It is hard to put a price on happiness, but it sometimes must be done.

RETIRE TO A SECOND CAREER

Do you have a job waiting for you? Remember, if you are considering early retirement, it's easy to talk casually about "resting up" for a while and then getting a new job. Sure it happens. But those who do not have a highly marketable skill could run into a difficult time in a period of high unemployment.

If you are in your 50s or older and do not have a job waiting for you, be wary of retiring early unless you have sufficient reserves to make additional income unnecessary: you might find it's awfully hard to find the new job you now take for granted.

If you are considering early retirement without plans to take another job, full- or part-time, then: what?

Are you really ready for all the leisure you'll find you have? Can you fill your time with community service, educational opportunities, hobbies, travel, sports, cards—whatever?

It sounds easy to do, but it isn't for many retirees.

Remember how many years you will have ahead if you retire early and make sure, by advance planning, that you can make them active and busy years.

Retire early if you can enjoy your later years more, free of financial worries and free of boredom. Stay on the job if you aren't sure you can.

TAKING THE DECISION

Every man or woman approaching retirement must make the decision to retire at 65 (or earlier) or go past 65 on a basis of individual circumstances.

The first and perhaps biggest question is: Do you need to continue working?

For example, are you paying off a mortgage and need to continue receiving a regular paycheck to do it comfortably? Do you still have a child or children in college and need your regular wages or salary to meet steadily climbing costs? Do you have some other important financial need that can best be met by continuing on your regular job beyond 65? Under such circumstances, the right to work on can be a relief.

If regular work is such a habit for you that the very thought of breaking it by retiring is a psychological problem, then perhaps working on beyond 65 is your answer. But remember in the long run the substitution of new things—work and play and just plain relaxing—may be better for you. If you feel that you must fill your time with work at a regular job, the law allows you to do so beyond 65.

On the other hand, consider this: the longer you go on, the harder it will be to retire—and someday you will have to. It is easier to change a lifestyle at an active 65 than at 70. You will adapt more easily to the things you would enjoy doing but haven't had an opportunity to do, and it will be easier to slip into a new, less arduous job if you want to supplement your retirement pay.

Before you decide, try doing the following: with the help of your employee benefits office at work and perhaps someone in the nearest Social Security office find out whether staying on the job beyond age 65 would substantially increase your eventual retirement benefits. For some, particularly those who have been jobless over long periods and have changed jobs frequently so that years of service for one employer haven't accumulated sufficiently, working beyond 65 could be a step toward a more adequate income in retirement.

RETIREMENT CHECKLIST

If you are considering early retirement, try answering these questions:

- Do you have something definite you want to do after early retirement? Is there something you have always wanted to do that you can undertake in your late 50's or early 60's? A second, deeply satisfying career, perhaps?
- Can you earn enough or have you saved enough to bridge the financial gap between what you will get as a pension if you retire early and the full amount that you'd get at 65?
- Have you factored in inflation? In retirement you'll need besides social security and your pension additional income. Keep in mind that if inflation holds steady at its 1993 rate—only 2.6%—$1,000 of today's dollars will be worth less than $500 in 2014. People age 60 today have a life expectancy of over 20 years.
- Have you planned sufficiently for early retirement? With your spouse and other members of your family? Remembering that planning for retirement at 65 should begin five to ten years before that?
- Financially, are major obligations (mortgages, children's education, installment credit and the like) paid off or under control?
- Have you thought about medical and hospital insurance between the time you leave your job and group plans and when you will become eligible for Medicare?
- Are you sure that early retirement will make you and your spouse—and all of your family—happier? That you really want it?

If you answer "no" to any of these questions, you should probably be doing more thinking about early retirement; perhaps you aren't ready for it.

Think about what changes you will have to make for your "no" answers to become "yes."

DON'T LEAVE DETAILS UNTIL LAST DAYS

"I'll have plenty of time to take care of retirement details when I retire. I'm busy now ..."

Many who retire regret saying—or thinking—something like that. Putting off detail work can lead to long delays in collecting Social Security or enjoying the potential benefits of retirement.

Advance planning for retirement should begin in your 40s, certainly no later than your early to mid-50s.

Now more than ever before, careful financial planning is necessary to acquire the assets needed to assure a comfortable and happy retirement. This can't be put off until you are 60 or over.

Generally, a combined pension program and Social Security will yield about 60% of your pre-retirement income. You may be able to live on less after your retire, but you probably will need a supplementary income to avoid a lowered standard of living.

In your 40s and 50s, concentrate on financing retirement years. In your 50s, begin giving more serious thought to what you want in retirement, how you would like to spend your time, where you will live and what adjustments you might have to make. You should think in specific ways about retirement—and if you are married, the planning should be done jointly. In your 50s, you should have a good idea of what you're going to do in your retirement.

In your early 60s, you must begin thin[k]ing about when you will retire—at 65? Earlier reduced benefits? Or later?

If you're thinking about retiring early, ch[eck] with your Social Security office to find out [how] much you'll forfeit in benefits, and with your c[om]pany personnel office to find out how your pen[sion] will be affected. Retiring at 62 could cost a[bout] 20% of the benefits you'd be due if you worke[d to] age 65.

Before you retire start checking on the do[cu]ments you will need to claim Social Security b[ene]fits: Social Security card and that of your spo[use.] Proofs of ages of both of you, preferably birth [cer]tificates? Your marriage license? Get them tog[eth]er and in order.

Decide on pension options, medical insura[nce] needs and options for handling mortgage or o[ther] financial obligations that will continue after re[tire]ment.

Decide, also, on whether automobiles and ap[pli]ances should be replaced while your income i[s at] maximum; it's generally a good idea to repl[ace] appliances over ten years old. And consider y[our] basic clothing needs.

Above all, begin developing retirement inter[ests] and activities. If married, these should be b[oth] individual and joint—too much togethern[ess] sometimes can be a problem.

In your 60s, you should be just about set [for] retirement.

JUST BEFORE YOU RETIRE, DO THIS

When your retirement time is approaching, here are some things you should do:

- Have a medical checkup while you are still covered by your company's medical program; it will save you money.

- Register with your Social Security office about three months in advance of your retirement date. It takes that long to process applications. Your spouse should go with you. Take the documents you need, including a copy of your last two W-2 tax forms, the withholding statement, and your spouse's tax papers if both of you are working.

- Check with former employers to find out whether you might be due partial pensions based on their contributions to pension plans in your behalf when you were employed. Vesting plans vary. Many who retire lose money because they neglect to check with former employers.

- Retirement benefits are available under some conditions to war veterans with limited incomes, or to widows of veterans. To qualify, veterans must be permanently or totally disabled due either to a service or non-service injury. If you think you might qualify, check with your nearest Veterans' Administration office.

- Most important, make realistic plans for day-to-day living in retirement. You should have estimates of what your financial needs will be for living costs, housing, insurance, health care, transportation, utilities, clothing, recreation and miscellaneous costs. With retirement day approaching, go over them carefully; in inflationary times living cost estimates made earlier may no longer be accurate. In addition to estimates of what you'll need, reassess what you'll have.

- Sit down with a personnel officer of your company to work out exactly what your pension will be—and the options open to you in monthly benefits. If you elect to collect monthly checks payable only until you die, your income will be larger but a surviving spouse will be left without pension checks. An alternative is to take a lesser amount that will continue after the death of the retiree. There are a number of joint-life plans based on actuarial tables for life expectancy of the employee and his or her spouse. You should know your options.

- Also check with your company on how and when pension checks will come to you; what options are open to you on accrued vacation or sick leave time (often you can get a lump-sum payment); whether life insurance carries over or must be switched from a group plan to an individual policy and what could be done about continuing health and hospitalization insurance.

- If you are retiring but plan to continue to work in a second career, get in advance, a copy of the pamphlet "You Can Work and Still Get Social Security" available from your Social Security office.

In a nutshell, when you retire, be ready. Know what retirement will mean and how you will have to accommodate to it.

WHEN YOU RETIRE

So you've retired. What then?

Your advance planning should have given you an answer to that question. However, here are things you should consider:

- If you have received a lump-sum payment from a qualified pension or profit-sharing plan, talk to someone at your bank or in a conservative brokerage or financial house about how it best can be used to meet your future needs. Don't consider the big check a windfall, and go on a spending spree. Remember, it's taxable money. You may avoid an immediate tax when you have higher income by transferring the money to an Individual Retirement Account (IRA) within 60 days.

- If you enrolled in Social Security three months before retirement, your first check should arrive about the third day of the month after you retire. Don't worry if it is late, Social Security is slow-moving. But you can count on your first check including all that's due you from retirement on.

- If after retirement, you may be willing and able to continue to work. Depending upon restrictions in your pension plan many retirees are able to continue full- or part-time employment. Check with your personnel or State employment office.

Retirement — 55, 65 or 70?

● Medicare provides hospital coverage after an annual deductible and a certain percentage of medical expenses after another deductible. Chapter 6 provides details of the provisions of both Hospital and Medical coverage by Medicare. These are subject to change by Congressional action. There are supplemental insurance policies you may buy. Check their benefits carefully before you buy.

● Your tax position changes with retirement. Social Security benefits are taxable if your adjusted gross income plus non-taxable interest and half of your Social Security benefit is more than a base amount (the base for an individual is $25,000—for a couple filing jointly it is $32,000), but part or all of your pension will be subject to income taxes. So will income you may have from part-time or other work, and from most other sources. Unless you take another regular job, you won't have money withheld to cover continuing taxes. Be prepared to handle more tax work—and tax payments—on your own. If you have any questions, call the nearest Internal Revenue Service office for answers.

● If you have your savings for retirement in growth and tax-deferred investments, check with your banker or broker about the advisability of changes to income and security accounts.

● Consider ways to cut costs. Does your auto insurer offer a premium rate to drivers of retirement age who do not use cars to drive to work? Some do. If your car is more than four years old, check with your agent about dropping the collision insurance in your policy; it mightn't be worth its cost to you. And if you plan to buy a new car, check on insurance rates for the cars you're interested in: rates differ from model to model.

● Reassess the adequacy of your home insurance every year. With inflation, repair and replacement costs are rising year to year. Be sure you are sufficiently protected against losses from fire or other hazards. Check with your life insurance agent on whether you can convert your present coverage to a paid-up policy and save on further premiums. It's sometimes possible but it might not be in your best interest.

● If you want to work, though perhaps not as hard or as long hours, there are agencies in most counties or cities that help older workers find part-time or full-time employment. Any local agency that works with older people can refer you to one. You may also register with an employment agency that furnishes temporary help if you have a marketable job experience. Also, want ads in your local newspaper are important for leads to jobs open to retirees—or that can be filled as easily by older workers as well as a younger.

● If you don't want a job but want to keep busy, investigate local volunteer service opportunities. Volunteers are in short supply everywhere.

● Don't try to adapt yourself overnight to your new life and your changed circumstances. Go at it slowly and carefully, remembering that retirement is not an end but a beginning.

● Check into recreation, education, civic activities—even politics—and community service that offer enough in the way of a new opportunity to provide a sound basis for a new life in retirement.

WOMEN LIVE LONGER

It's something we don't like to think about and sit down and talk about. Still, we must face the fact that an estimated 85% of all married women in the United States will be widowed.

Six out of ten women in the pre-retirement age group 55 to 64 are married while four out of ten are either widowed, divorced or have never married. For the age group 65 to 74 somewhat less are still married.

Both groups, in planning for their retirement, face similar concerns and some that are different.

For both, understanding one's financial situation is of fundamental importance.

Women who never married or have been widowed or divorced have had some experience in handling their financial affairs, while some married women left these details to their husbands. There are of course many who are as able as their husbands to list family assets, debts and otherwise summarize their financial position.

MOM'S WORKING AND DAD'S NOT

In today's work environment, with company downsizing and early retirement, the expectations of many families have been affected. Many men find themselves in retirement much earlier than anticipated. Meanwhile, their wives continue to work. This creates a new dynamic in the home and in the husband-wife relationship that can be difficult for both to adjust to.

Many successfully make the transition. Those that do approach their unexpected new circumstances as an opportunity—even if not welcomed—to start a new career or pursue long put-off objectives. There is a greater need for planning, though, both financial and otherwise. The many chapters in this book can help.

ASK YOURSELF QUESTIONS

Women's longevity makes it necessary for them to face that mirror-mirror on the wall:

- How many years can I expect to live with my spouse after retirement?
- How many years will one of us be likely to live alone?
- Whether married or single, what is my life expectancy?

Life Expectancy					
	Male			Female	
Age	Expectancy	Years	Age	Expectancy	Years
50	75.5	25.5	50	79.6	29.6
55	76.7	21.7	55	80.5	25.5
60	78.2	18.2	60	81.7	21.7
65	80.0	15.0	65	83.2	18.2

YOU'VE HEARD THIS BEFORE... PLAN AHEAD!

By now you've bought insurance, made your will, may have even discussed retirement with spouse, friend, family. Have you, however, been realistic and honest?

With age, married or not, comes death of beloved ones.

"A" means one; "lone" means solitary. Together they mean being apart from anything or anyone else—without any other person. But "alone" can have several connotations according to your point of view. A person whose adult life has been spent as a single person may consider being alone to be their natural state—the way they always are used to being. This person has the experience of being independent, of having a unique identity, of having a self-relationship. Decisions and actions are made without the need to consult another. A majority of us acquire a mate early in our adult life. Along with the marriage partner and probable family, we develop a sense of interdependence. We share decisions and responsibilities and our identity is strongly and inevitably intertwined with our partner. Our marriage and family life offers a source of love, security, emotional support, and companionship.

What happens when a person who has spent their adult life in partnership with another is faced with the reality of being alone. The prospect of your becoming widowed, of ending your life experience with your marriage partner, is almost beyond thought. Still, you would be far better off by giving serious thought to how you can at least be somewhat prepared for that eventuality.

The purpose of this section is to provide a guide for that thinking. You can plan and prepare many of your affairs with your partner as you always have, and do it more securely and easily than if you were alone and under stress and emotional upheaval. In the following pages we will discuss such subjects as the importance of a valid and detailed will, management of your property, your financial and legal affairs, and the importance of insurance, particularly health insurance. We will also discuss the emotional aspects of dying, death, and widowhood, the feelings of a dying person, "death with dignity," the importance of grief, and the changes and adjustments that take place in the surviving spouse's life as a new identity is developed.

Being prepared is not an indication that you are preparing for the imminent death of your partner. The chances are that you have many happy years together ahead of you. But if an accidental death or fatal illness should occur, at least you will be in a position to carry on with and manage your life.

BEING PREPARED

"How can anyone be prepared for widowhood?"

It may not be possible to be ready for the wrenching shock of learning that your spouse is

dying or has died. One thing you can do in regard is to understand something of the emoti you are feeling and realize that it is good to grie Grief is the way our minds become reconcile giving up a loved one.

And we may feel other things besides grief. may feel guilt—guilty for not having done cer things when our husband or wife was alive. may feel angry—we are angry at being abando and left all alone, at having to be without the aw ness of where certain things are or what needs to done. We may feel lost—the old routines and terns of living are gone. There is no one to breakfast with in the morning, and no one to tall at night. We are at a loss about what to do or wh to go. We may feel despair—despair so deep we want to die. There will also be many pai days, when holidays come, or anniversaries birthdays. We think back to what was and now no longer, and we feel terribly down.

AFTERWARD

The months following the death of someone love are difficult and critical times in our l They are difficult, because we have to deal with kinds of emotions, and without the help of so one with whom we used to share many of our w ries and cares. They are critical times because are starting out on our own to make a new life ourselves. We will have to learn new skills, things we never dreamed of doing, make frie and find new ways to spend our time usefully.

No one can prevent this time in our life fr being painful. People can help and will help, if let them.

We may need the help of an attorney or a fir cial counselor for legal and monetary matt There will be many matters to take care of inv

ing taxes, property, inheritance, Social Security, insurance and the like. It will cost us some money to get help with such things, but is may cost us more not to. Very soon, after the funeral, we will want to take care of these matters: 1) processing the will, 2) freeing bank accounts, 3) changing title on property, car, stock, etc., 4) settling unpaid bills, while keeping accurate and complete records, 5) applying for Social Security funeral benefits, and 6) filing life insurance claims.

Other affairs that we must take care of but that we need not be concerned with for awhile are income taxes, budgeting, seeing that our own will is as we want it, inheritance and estate taxes, and possibly others if you have minor children or dependents. We should keep in close communication with a knowledgeable friend or our attorney to be sure all necessary tasks are accomplished.

During the period after the death of our spouse we may also need the emotional support that counseling, by a psychologist or minister, can give, particularly if we find that our grieving does not lessen after about six weeks. But most of all we need to help ourselves. We need to find the power within ourselves to start a new life and to begin to discover who we are, what our potentials are, and what possibilities lie before us.

HINGS TO DO

Planning for both married and single should begin in the mid-50's or earlier. Be not discouraged if you are well past that point. Only gain can come from starting—NOW!

SSETS AND DEBTS

Assess your assets and debits as soon as possible. Summarize your whole family financial position. This is difficult for women who customarily left the handling of these matters of business entirely to a husband.

For all women, now is the time to understand your financial status. Don't wait for retirement. If you set your mind to it and seek advice you'll find it far less bewildering than you might have thought. It's just a matter of attention and faith in yourself.

Looking ahead to retirement, even if it's a decade or more away, husbands and wives should work together to prepare and maintain a careful inventory of what the family has—of all assets— and what they owe. They should consider together all insurance policies (life, health and hospitaliza-

---

Expand your interests, meet interesting people — develop new friends.

Take a class—at your local community college or adult educational center.

Join a club—clubs are organized for almost any interest.

Attend church—and participate in its activities—you'll never be lonesome.

Volunteer—the first person you help is yourself.

Politics—make a contribution to our political life and work with active people interested in public issues.

Travel—check with Elderhostel (75 Federal Street, Boston, MA 02110-1941) or Interhostel (University of New Hampshire, 6 Garrison Ave., Durham, NH 03824-3529) for group travel worldwide sponsored by American colleges. Once you participate in a session, you'll be back year after year. Send for their catalogs

Evergreen Travel Club—members host each other in their own homes (404 North Galena Ave., L-20, Dixon, IL 61021).

Join your local museum—and participation its activities. They need volunteers.

Be active in your alumni group—see old friends and make new ones.

Your local school—it could use your services.

---

tion, accident, household, auto or whatever) and list them, noting the names of companies, numbers of the policies, names of agents and where the policies are kept. And they should make and update as necessary legal wills, one for each partner, and note where they can be found.

Too many husbands think they do wives a favor by assuming responsibilities for handling bank accounts, bill payments, debts, investments and other money matters; they seem to think of this as a husband's job.

Instead of a favor, those who shut wives out of financial affairs may be creating a major problem for spouses who might suddenly be confronted with a need to cope responsibly with such matters

The result could be headaches and heartaches for a spouse in a time of crisis—and possibly extra financial costs

Women must have the knowledge of family affairs and experience in handling day-to-day financial matters if—in an emergency—they are to handle the chores alone. Shared handling of financial matters will make lone decisions easier.

Review Financial Matters

❑ Do both you and your spouse review together your family's financial obligations and resources?

❑ Are both you and your spouse aware of where your money is kept (bank, investments, property, etc.) and the status of major policies such as insurance?

❑ Are complete financial records, including names of your lawyer, insurance agent, bank, and broker, filed in an organized manner that husband, wife or relative can refer to?

❑ Are children involved in money matters that affect them? Are they, or someone you trust, in a position to help manage your family's finances should the need arise?

If you do these things, each of you will have a good idea of how the family stands financially. While this will not ease the grief, it can reduce confusion and unnecessary strain at a very bad time of life.

WILL YOUR WIFE BE FINANCIALLY SECURE IF YOU DIE?

That's another question you have to think about together. Is the husband's life insurance adequate? If he is retired, would his pension terminate with his death? If he is still working, would his pension program provide for his widow if he dies before retirement? What help would Social Security be, either way? And would there be adequate health and hospital insurance?

KNOW YOUR PENSION

Many working men—and women—do not know enough about their pension plans. They know, only vaguely, what they can expect in monthly payments after retirement at age 65. They have

not read, or have forgotten, the fine print in sion material furnished by employers.

It is a good idea to take a close look at pe plans to find answers to the questions we aske

CHECK INSURANCE

You should check on what would happen to health and hospital insurance coverage, partic ly under group insurance programs. If there any provisions for extending coverage, explor possibilities.

About life insurance: It's a good idea to re the amount of coverage you have in the ligh inflating cost of living. What might have I adequate coverage when policies were taken might be inadequate now.

This can be summarized briefly: Although partner can live more cheaply than two, there be questions whether the amount of incon widow can expect from a pension program insurance payments would supplement So Security sufficiently to assure her a comforta worry-free life.

Savings and additional planning now could e her problems.

CHECK BENEFITS

Familiarize yourself with Social Security mate available on racks at the nearest office to you. don't have to wait until approaching retirem age: if you are fully covered and become disab or die, the details of this program can be import at any age. So: check it out.

For widows with nest eggs from savings a insurance, what they receive from Social Secu is often enough to provide for a modest, relativ comfortable life. Without the backup of p planned savings and adequate insurance, bud tightening could take away some of the comforts

DECISIONS WIDOWS WILL HAVE TO MAKE

Many women find that after the death of a husba they face, in addition to loneliness and grief, wo ries about budgeting and managing money, alon with a lot of other problems that were the hu band's responsibility before his death.

For some, the necessity of tackling such ne things is therapeutic. For others, it is added stra and more unhappiness.

HANDLING MONEY

One of the first and toughest decisions a widow must make is what to do with the money from insurance policies and from her husband's estate generally. She may suddenly have what seems to be a great deal of capital.

If she is inexperienced in handling capital, she could feel overwhelmed. It is a good idea for a husband and wife to plan well in advance what can be done. Sound guidance is important—at any time.

In regard to family savings and investment programs, be wary, set clear objectives based on projected annual budget needs, get expert counseling, but avoid letting capital stay idle and unproductive because of uncertainties about what should be done and what should not.

Annuities can provide an assured income for life, but they limit flexibility. Once funds are committed, they cannot be retrieved or shifted.

Flexibility is necessary because of inflation and because needs vary. It's a good idea to explore the variety of investment possibilities early, in connection with pre-retirement planning, and establish a sound program that provides a basis for the use of insurance and other money if or when a wife is widowed.

SOCIAL SECURITY BENEFITS FOR WOMEN

Changes made in the Social Security law in 1983 added additional benefits for women. Benefits will be continued for surviving divorced spouses and disabled widows and widowers who remarry, after the first year of eligibility.

An eligible divorced spouse age 62 or over whose divorce has been in effect at least two years can become eligible for benefits based on the earnings of a former spouse who is eligible for retirement, regardless of whether the former spouse has retired or applied for benefits.

THE RETIREMENT EQUITY ACT

The 1984 Retirement Equity Act makes it easier for women to receive retirement benefits under pension plans, either their husband's or their own.

The Act requires that a spouse would have to give written permission before an employee could choose a plan that would stop payments upon the employee's death instead of continuing payments to the surviving spouse.

The Act requires the payment of a pension to the spouse of a worker who was fully vested in a pension plan or had become eligible for the plan after working a certain number of years if the worker dies before reaching retirement age. The surviving spouse would receive the pension benefits at the earliest retirement age under his plan.

The Act lowers the age from 25 to 21 at which workers must be allowed to participate in a pension plan.

The Act requires the pension plan to count the years of an employee's service from the time the person turns 18 in calculating when the employee had worked long enough to be eligible for a pension at retirement.

The Act would bar pension plans from counting a year maternity or paternity leave as a break in service.

Employees who have worked fewer than five years would be allowed to take five years off without losing pension credit for earlier service.

The Act authorizes a Court to award a person part of their former spouse's pension as part of a divorce settlement.

DON'T SIGN PENSION WAIVER UNLESS YOU UNDERSTAND THE CHOICES.

Guide for Women on Social Security

Women of all ages might want to write for a free copy of "Social Security: What Every Woman Absolutely Needs to Know," a publication from the American Association of Retired Persons.

This publication, produced in cooperation with the Social Security Administration, helps women to understand the Social Security system and what their benefits are. It also explains how to apply for benefits and how to appeal a denial.

For a single copy, write to AARP, Fulfillment, 601 E Street, NW, Washington, DC 20049. Ask for publication No. D14117.

WOMEN IN RETIREMENT: A CHECKLIS

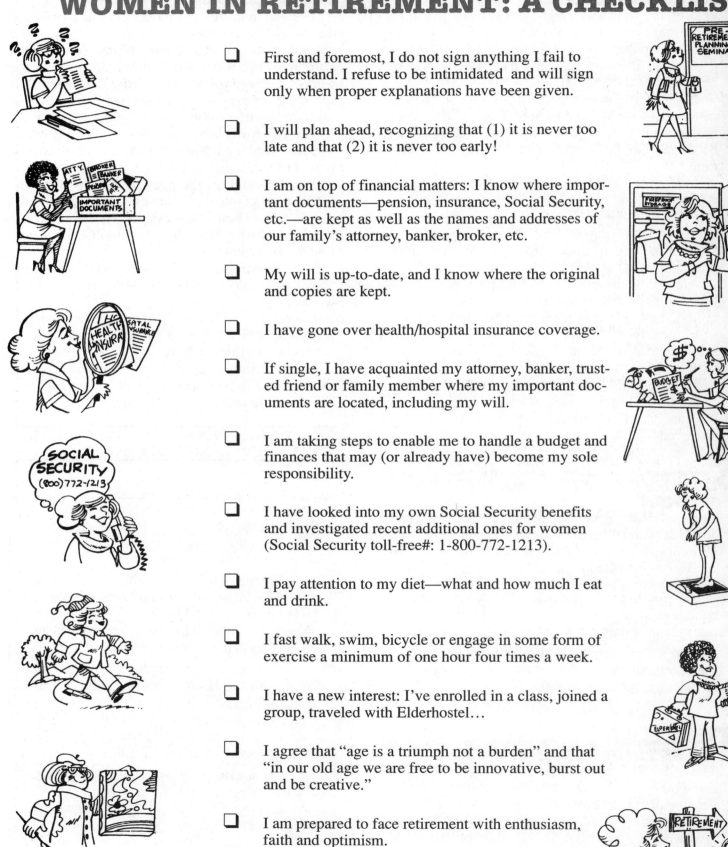

- ❑ First and foremost, I do not sign anything I fail to understand. I refuse to be intimidated and will sign only when proper explanations have been given.

- ❑ I will plan ahead, recognizing that (1) it is never too late and that (2) it is never too early!

- ❑ I am on top of financial matters: I know where important documents—pension, insurance, Social Security, etc.—are kept as well as the names and addresses of our family's attorney, banker, broker, etc.

- ❑ My will is up-to-date, and I know where the original and copies are kept.

- ❑ I have gone over health/hospital insurance coverage.

- ❑ If single, I have acquainted my attorney, banker, trusted friend or family member where my important documents are located, including my will.

- ❑ I am taking steps to enable me to handle a budget and finances that may (or already have) become my sole responsibility.

- ❑ I have looked into my own Social Security benefits and investigated recent additional ones for women (Social Security toll-free#: 1-800-772-1213).

- ❑ I pay attention to my diet—what and how much I eat and drink.

- ❑ I fast walk, swim, bicycle or engage in some form of exercise a minimum of one hour four times a week.

- ❑ I have a new interest: I've enrolled in a class, joined a group, traveled with Elderhostel…

- ❑ I agree that "age is a triumph not a burden" and that "in our old age we are free to be innovative, burst out and be creative."

- ❑ I am prepared to face retirement with enthusiasm, faith and optimism.

The delight I feel when any one of them wraps his [o]r her arms around me, gives me a BIG hug, and [s]ays, "Hi, grandpa!"…it's priceless."
> **—A Los Angeles grandparent**

[D]ID YOU KNOW…?

- On the first Sunday after Labor Day each year, Americans around the country celebrate National Grandparents' Day.
- In the United States alone there are now at least 60 million grandparents.
- Nearly 5 million U.S. children live in extended families that include one or more grandparents in their household.
- 6.4% of grandparents are under the age of 45; 37.8% are 65 or older.

As the numbers above suggest, close to one in [f]our Americans are grandparents. Chances are, if [y]ou are not one yourself, you know someone who [i]s. There was also a time in your life when YOU [w]ere a grandchild, hoping for a moment of your [g]randparents' time.

So what do these facts mean for you today? [O]bviously, it will affect you most if you are now a [g]randparent, for this is one "job" you will never [r]etire from.

Grandparenting is both a joy and a [r]esponsibility, which links your working days with [y]our retired ones. It provides a sense of continuity [a]nd stability throughout the years, both for you and [y]our grandchild. It is a way for you to keep feeling [v]ital and important, to make a contribution that is [m]eaningful for all concerned. It is "a relatively [p]ure form of love and affection" providing you [w]ith companionship, pleasure and pride.

[W]HAT DOES IT MEAN TO BE A GRANDPARENT?

[T]here is much grandparents can do to enrich their [g]randchildren's experience…. Grandparents [s]hould be good listeners… communication is nine-[t]enths of a good relationship…. They also play an [i]mportant role in heightening the children's sense [o]f security…. They are symbols of longevity and [t]he extent of the human lifespan."
> **—Bill Bookman**

GRANDCHILDREN: THE SPICE IN YOUR LIFE

You will certainly be making a contribution to your grandchildren's lives—in fact, a recent study found that grandparents are second only to parents in the influence they have on children's lives—but in doing so, you will also be adding to your own sense of purpose and self-worth. It feels good to be a good grandparent, just as it feels good to be a good worker or community leader or parent.

Your grandkids can add a little spice to your life, just as you can to theirs. And you can pass on family traditions and history to them in the process.

With the increase in single-parent and two-income families, you may even find yourself playing an important or stabilizing role in the upbringing of your children's children.

Grandparents can be a big help by watching their grandchildren during those couple of hours each day after they're back from school, but before their parents have arrived home from work.

STAYING IN TOUCH

You can make a great difference in your grandchild's life, just by making a simple phone call, or sending a picture postcard. Send postcards to your grandchildren even before they can read, because the parents read them to them. They love to receive postcards addressed just to them.

Another idea is to call up and speak to the grandchild and when the grandchild says, "Do you want to speak to my mother?" say "No, I just called to speak to you."

BRIDGING THE MILES: LONG-DISTANCE GRANDPARENTING

You may be concerned that you live too far away from your grandchildren to be an active grandparent. With modern communication and transportation being what they are, the miles can be easily bridged. After all, your efforts—as simply as sending a birthday card, calling to ask about your grandchild's schoolwork or activities, or telling the child a story about your own life and past—will long remain in the memories of your grandchildren.

One of the most important things a grandparent can do for a grandchild is simply to be there for him or her (whether this be on the phone or in person), to listen and understand.

Remember, a grandparent usually has a different role than that of a parent. Most grandchildren view their grandparents as a refuge from the daily demands of a disciplined home. Grandma and Grandpa can give kids something their parents may not be able to give enough of, yet one of the things they need most: time.

This type of positive grandparent-grandchild relationship can be fostered with just a little extra effort on your part, whether you are one or one thousand miles away. A few minutes spent on the phone now will pay off handsomely later, in the well-being of your grandchildren. And this, in turn, will make YOU feel better.

There is yet another possibility for grandparents who want to spend concentrated quality time with their grandchildren. You can invite your grandchild on a holiday or camp stay. There are organizations that specialize in arranging trips with grandchildren that can help make these arrangements.

WHAT TO DO WITH YOUR GRANDCHILDREN

❑ Contact your grandchild as often as possible. Visit if you live nearby or are able to travel. Make a phone call or send a postcard or videotape of yourself if you live far away.

❑ Accept your grandchildren as they are. Don't try to mold them to your own vision of the perfect grandchild.

❑ Encourage and answer questions. Treat them as important people and respect their thoughts and opinions.

❑ Take risks. The doorway to loving time with your grandchildren is blocked only by apprehension.

❑ Be your grandchildren's playmate and friend. Set aside your crossword puzzle or book and do what they want to do. Let them set the agenda.

❑ Take your grandchildren to the zoo, a museum, the ballgame, or the movies. They'll remember the shared experience for a long time to come.

❑ Provide a link with the past; show your grandchild pictures of you as a child.

❑ Create memories and traditions. Tell your grandchild about your family history and traditions or your own childhood. Consider creating an oral or written history to hand down to your descendants.

❑ Show your grandchild that getting older is a happy time in life.

❑ Share triumphs as well as misfortunes.

WHAT IF YOUR GRANDCHILDREN ARE UNDER YOUR OWN CARE?

Perhaps your concern is not that you don't see your grandchildren enough, but rather that you see them more than you had originally bargained for. You might even live with your grandchildren or be their primary caregivers. This is not an uncommon circumstance in the 1990's, and can admittedly be trying at times, but if you find yourself in such a situation, it can only help to look at the bright side.

You are not alone. An estimated 4.7 million children live with one or both of their grandparents in some capacity, and 1.1 million of these children are actually being raised by their grandparents rather than their parents. Whether this is a result of choice or obligation, you should know that there are plenty of others just like you, and that support networks exist to assist you with legal, financial, and child-care concerns.

Chapter Fourteen

The value of your extraordinary commitment to your grandchildren should not be underestimated. It will probably be hard work, but it's worth it. If you need help or support, don't hesitate to contact the Grandparent Information Center in Washington, DC, or other organizations who understand concerns such as yours. And remember that your efforts will live on in the lives and minds of your growing grandchildren!

Remember, also, to take care of yourself. Your health and well-being are critical to the health and well-being of your grandchildren.

WHAT IF YOU HAVE NO GRAND-CHILDREN OF YOUR OWN?

You might be surprised to find out that there are still plenty of opportunities for you to work with children. In fact, even if you do have grandchildren of your own, you may still want to lend a hand or an ear to other children in your community, in effect as a "surrogate" grandparent.

Depending on the level of the commitment you want to make, you have several options to choose from.

The simplest would be to volunteer at a local school or hospital, where your many years of experience will be your most valuable asset. Your work can be of almost any capacity—teaching, counseling, discussing, or simply sharing ideas and thoughts with today's youth.

To arrange this, you can contact any local volunteer clearinghouse, or the Corporation for National Service, which runs both the National Senior Service Corps and the Retired Senior Volunteer Program.

WORDS OF WISDOM

"Grandparenting is an art. Its principles can be stated in generalized words, but the practice has to be learned in the doing. The circumstances of each family are different, and the family members are unique personalities."
—Bill Bookman, syndicated columnist

"Perhaps grandparents' most important function is as a reserve, to be there in case of need. Grandparents are the family National Guard, on stand-by duty to be called out in emergencies.... It's a positive thing that there are no strict rules on how a grandparent should behave. It gives them a lot of flexibility. They can serve a variety of functions precisely because it is so ambiguous."
—Gunhild Hagestad, a Northwestern University sociologist

"It's a positive thing that there are no strict rules on how a grandparent should behave. It gives them a lot of flexibility. They can serve a variety of functions precisely because it is so ambiguous."
—Gunhild Hagestad

TIME SPENT WITH YOUR GRANDCHILDREN...

...WILL PLEASE YOUR GRANDCHILDREN...

...AND *YOU* TOO!

Grandparenting

Another option is the Family Friends program of the National Council on the Aging. This federally-sponsored program recruits older people to provide respite for families with seriously ill children, often leading to a grandparent-grandchild type relationship forming between the child and the volunteer.

As a Family Friend, you agree to spend a certain amount of time with the sick child, to relieve the immediate family of their 24-hour commitment to their loved one.

If you are willing to make a more seriou commitment, you might want to consider applyin to the U.S. government's Peace Corps or Vist programs. With the Peace Corps, you can reques to work with children abroad, teaching anythin from personal hygiene to the harvesting of crops t language and communication skills. Vista offer similar programs within the United States.

There is a host of other opportunities, al available to you for the asking. Contact any of th organizations listed below.

RESOURCES FOR GRANDPARENTS

National Council on the Aging
409 Third Street, SW, Suite 200
Washington, DC 20024
Telephone: (202) 479-6675
Sponsors the Family Friends program, which recruits older people to provide respite for families with sick children.

Foundation for Grandparenting
Arthur Kornhaber, M.D.
53 Principe de Paz
Santa Fe, NM 87505
Telephone: (505) 466-1029
Dr. Kornhaber, a psychiatrist, has recently published his fourth book on grandparenting, titled Grandparent Power, published by Crown Books. Send a self-addressed stamped envelope for information on the Foundation's numerous services and newsletter.

Grandparent Information Center
c/o American Association of Retired Persons
601 E Street, NW
Washington, DC 20049
Telephone: (202) 434-2296
Offers information and support to grandparents raising grandchildren.

Corporation for National Service
Senior Services Division
1100 Vermont Avenue, NW
Washington, DC 20525
Telephone: (800) 424-8867
Sponsors the Senior Companion Program, Retired Senior Volunteer Program, and Foster Grandparent Program.

Your local church, synagogue, library and social services agency will have additional information on resources in your community.

For More Information

Government publications: For a free listing of publications for sale write: Superintendent of Documents, U.S. Government Printing Office, P.O. Box 37194, Pittsburgh, PA 15250-7954.

For a list of free booklets on aging write: Publications, Administration on Aging, OHDS/HHS, Washington, DC 20201.

For your free copy of the Consumers Information Catalog, listing over 200 consumer publications, send a postcard to: Consumers Information Catalog, Pueblo, CO 81009.

College aid: For a worksheet to help figure out how much financial aid your child would qualify for, ask a high school guidance office for the College Board's free brochure, "Meeting College Costs."

The Federal Student Aid Information Center has a free booklet, *The Student Guide: Five Federal Financial Aid Programs.* You can order it by calling toll-free, 1-800-433-3243, or by writing to the Center at P.O. Box 84, Washington, DC 20044.

Debt problems: The non-profit Consumer Credit Counseling Service, with over 600 offices nationwide, offers free or low-cost budget planning and assistance in working out financial difficulties. Check local yellow pages, call toll-free (1-800-388-2227) or write to the National Foundation for Consumer Credit, 8611 2nd Avenue, Suite 100, Silver Spring, MD 20910.

Financial planners: If you need a financial planner (see page 11), you can find one through two industry associations. The National Association of Personal Financial Advisors will send you a list of its members in your area. They are fee-only planners who have at least two years' experience and at least one professional designation. Call or write NAPFA at 1130 Lake Cook Rd., Suite 150, Buffalo Grove, IL 60089, 1-708-537-7722

The International Association for Financial Planning will send you a free list of planners who have demonstrated experience and knowledge of the profession. For a copy, write to IAFP, 2 Concourse Parkway, Suite 800, Atlanta, GA 30328 or call 1-404-395-1605.

Exercise: The President's Council on Physical Fitness has prepared a guide, *Walking for Exercise and Pleasure,* that includes illustrated warm-up exercises and advice on how far, how fast, and how often to walk for best results. Send $1 to Consumer Information Center-3C, P.O. Box 100, Pueblo, CO 81002 and ask for Publication 109Z.

Pensions: For general information about pensions, write to the American Association of Retired Persons, Fulfillment Department, at 601 E Street, NW, Washington, DC 20049 and ask for publication D-13533, *A Guide to Understanding Your Pension Plan.*

The basics of pensions are explained in clear terms in *Your Pension: Things You Should Know About Your Pension Plan* by the Pension Benefit Guaranty Corp. Among the subjects: What may happen to your retirement funds if you change jobs frequently and the implications of lump-sum distributions from a retirement plan vs. annuity payments. For a copy, send $1 to the Superintendent of Documents, Government Printing Office, P.O. Box 37194, Pittsburgh, PA 15250-7954. You'll need to mention the GPO stock number: 068-000-00003-3. Or call 1-202-783-3238.

If your employer can't furnish a copy of your pension plan's annual statement, you can get one from the U.S. Department of Labor. Call 1-202-219-8771. You'll need to know your employer's name, address, and federal tax identification number (it should be on your W-2 wage statement), and the name of the pension plan. Cost: 15¢ a page.

Insurance: For free copies of the Insurance Consumer's Bill of Rights and Responsibilities, by the Consumer Insurance Interest Group, write to the National Association of Professional Insurance Agents, 400 N. Washington Street, Alexandria, Virginia 22314.

For a brochure providing consumer information on life insurance, write to the American Council of Life Insurance, Company Services, 1001 Pennsylvania Ave., NW, Washington, DC 20004-2599.

A consortium of life, health, property and casualty insurers has a toll-free insurance help line. You can reach it at: 1-800-942-4242.

THE YEARS AHEAD

The National Institute of Health reports that most people are living longer and, when older, enjoying life much more.

Not too many years ago, there was an unfortunate concept that things ended abruptly at retirement age, 65 for most Americans, because, "one was old" at that age. We now know that in today's culture that is nonsense.

The truth of the matter is that if you reach age 65, you will have anywhere from 15 to 19 or more years of life ahead of you. As a male, you can expect to live to about 80 and as a female at least to 84.

The longevity today has prompted the National Institute of Health to note that there are three distinct "ages" after 65, roughly a decade apart and each with its different characteristics. In looking ahead to retirement, or if retired and planning for later years, it is interesting to consider the NIH findings.

According to the National Institute of Health:

The first "age"—from 65 to 75—is likely to show no substantial decline in capabilities. The NIH calls this period "young old," a continuation of midlife with only a slight drop in ability to take hikes, play golf or tennis or engage in other accustomed physical activities.

There are reams of data to demonstrate that when you are in your 60's or early 70's your ability to recall, remember, to reason, to calculate numbers will be virtually identical.

Some changes begin to show up in the second "age" from 75 to 85. Lives begin to slow down. We become less confident than we were before age 75.

After age 85 people concentrate more on making their lives comfortable and happy by relaxing more but remaining active by spending time with their friends, children and grandchildren.

IN CONCLUSION

Retirement is a time of change, growth, and adjustment. Sounds like a difficult time, doesn't it? Perhaps, but the best way to turn apprehension into confidence is by planning.

We hope that this book has helped you, and that you are looking forward to retirement with anticipation, good humor . . . and plans that are right for you.

Some final advice which we appreciate:

AFTER SEVENTY ...

Pamper the body,
Prod the soul
Accept limitations,
But play a role
Withdraw from the front,
But stay in the fight
Avoid isolation,
Keep in sight
Beware of reminiscing,
Except to a child
To forgetting proper names,
Be reconciled
Refrain from loquacity,
Be crisp and concise
And regard self-pity
As a cardinal vice.
— *Oliver Higgins Prouty*